Voting for Women

Dilemmas in American Politics

Series Editor: **L. Sandy Maisel,** *Colby College*

If the answers to the problems facing U.S. democracy were easy, politicians would solve them, accept credit, and move on. But certain dilemmas have confronted the American political system continuously. They defy solution; they are endemic to the system. Some can best be described as institutional dilemmas: How can the Congress be both a representative body and a national decision-maker? How can the president communicate with more than 250 million citizens effectively? Why do we have a two-party system when many voters are disappointed with the choices presented to them? Others are policy dilemmas: How do we find compromises on issues that defy compromise, such as abortion policy? How do we incorporate racial and ethnic minorities or immigrant groups into American society, allowing them to reap the benefits of this land without losing their identity? How do we fund health care for our poorest or oldest citizens?

Dilemmas such as these are what propel students toward an interest in the study of U.S. government. Each book in the *Dilemmas in American Politics Series* addresses a "real world" problem, raising the issues that are of most concern to students. Each is structured to cover the historical and theoretical aspects of the dilemma but also to explore the dilemma from a practical point of view and to speculate about the future. The books are designed as supplements to introductory courses in American politics or as case studies to be used in upper-level courses. The link among them is the desire to make the real issues confronting the political world come alive in students' eyes.

BOOKS IN THIS SERIES

Voting for Women

How the Public Evaluates Women Candidates

Kathleen A. Dolan
University of Wisconsin-Milwaukee

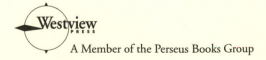
A Member of the Perseus Books Group

Dilemmas in American Politics

Copyright © 2004 by Westview Press, A Member of the Perseus Books Group

Published in the United States of America by Westview Press, A Member of the Perseus Books Group,
5500 Central Avenue, Boulder, Colorado 80301-2877, and in the United Kingdom by Westview Press,
12 Hid's Copse Road, Cumnor Hill, Oxford OX2 9JJ.

Find us on the world wide web at www.westviewpress.com

Westview Press books are available at special discounts for bulk purchases in the United States by cor-
porations, institutions, and other organizations. For more information, please contact the Special
Markets Department at the Perseus Books Group, 11 Cambridge Center, Cambridge, MA 02142, or
call (617) 252-5298, (800) 255-1514, or email j.mccrary@perseusbooks.com.

Library of Congress Cataloging-in-Publication Data

Dolan, Kathleen A.
 Voting for women : how the public evaluates women candidates /
Kathleen A. Dolan.
     p. cm. — (Dilemmas in American politics)
 Includes bibliographical references and index.
 ISBN 0-8133-4105-1 (hardcover : alk. paper) — ISBN 0-8133-9841-X (pbk. : alk. paper)
  1. Women political candidates—United States. I. Title. II. Series.
HQ1236.5.U6D64 2003
320'.082'0973—dc21

2003009391

The paper used in this publication meets the requirements of the American National Standard for Per-
manence of Paper for Printed Library Materials Z39.48–1984.

Typeface used in this text: 11-point Minion

10   9   8   7   6   5   4   3   2   1

This book is dedicated to
My family—Tom, Olivia, and Clayton
And to the guys at Providence College—
Jim, Bill, Mark, and Bob

Contents

4 **Who Votes for Women Candidates? Voter Demographics**   87
· ·

5 **Why Vote for Women Candidates? The Role of Issues**   113
· ·

6 **The Role of the Electoral Environment**   131
· ·

7 **Conclusions: The Role of Candidate
Sex in American Elections**   151
· ·

Tables and Figures

Tables

Figures

Acknowledgments

DURING THE SECOND SEMESTER of my first year in college, in Mark Hyde's Introduction to Political Analysis class, I received an assignment to evaluate a journal article on a topic that interested me. I chose "The Impact of Candidate Sex on Voter Choice" by Laurie Ekstrand and William Eckert (*Western Political Quarterly* 34 [1981]). That assignment began my work on a body of research on attitudes toward women candidates that includes my dissertation, several journal articles, and now this book. My thinking about women candidates has, I hope, evolved over the years. Regardless, I know that the debts, both intellectual and personal, that I owe to those who have helped me along this path are significant.

I am indebted to Barbara Burrell, Peggy Conway, Lynne Ford, and Karen O'Connor for a multitude of things. Each of them read and commented on the prospectus for this book, offering encouragement that it was an idea worth pursuing. But I owe each of them a greater debt for things large and small over the years. Peggy has served above and beyond the call over the years, continuing to read my work and to offer support and encouragement long after her official role as my dissertation chair ended. Barbara and Karen have been mentors and friends, offering advice and opportunities for professional growth over the years. Lynne has been my best friend for close to 20 years now, providing friendship, support, and the benefits of her recent experiences as a first-time book author. To each of them I say thank you.

In working on this manuscript, I have met a number of people from whose talent and advice I, and the project, have benefited. For early support of this project when it was in its infancy, I would like to acknowledge Dianne Bystrom, director of the Carrie Chapman Catt Center for Women and Politics at Iowa State University. Julie Prost, a graduate student at UWM, served as a wonderful research assistant, gathering data and providing research support. I would also like to thank Gilda Morales of the Center for the American Woman and Politics at Rutgers University for her help in tracking down information about women candidates. Ashley Grosse, formerly of the

National Election Study at the University of Michigan, went out of her way to help me on various aspects of this project, and I am grateful for her generosity. For financial support and release time, I thank Richard Meadows, Dean of the College of Letters and Science at University of Wisconsin Milwaukee; UWM's Graduate School Research Council award program; and the Women's Studies Faculty Fellows program. I thank Leo Weigman, my first editor at Westview Press, and Sandy Maisel, the series editor, for accepting the book for publication in the first place. I also extend thanks to Sandy and the anonymous reviewers for their careful reading of the manuscript and the thoughtful comments they provided. Steve Catalano, my editor at Westview, has been nothing but upbeat and supportive, making this a very enjoyable experience. I have to thank Steve particularly for a phone call in September 2002 that provided a much-needed kick in the pants. Others at Westview with whom I have worked, including Elisabeth Malzahn, Erica Lawrence, and Melissa Root, have also been extremely helpful and supportive.

This book is dedicated to two groups of people, my debts to whom are too numerous to catalog here. The first, Jim Carlson, Bill Hudson, Mark Hyde, and Bob Trudeau, were my undergraduate political science professors at Providence College. They are the people who first taught me what political science was all about, and they are the ones who encouraged me to think about it as a career. They even signed me up for my first membership in the APSA as a graduation gift. Over the years, they have been my teachers, my mentors, my role models, and, I am proud to say, my friends. To say that I wouldn't be doing what I do today without their help and guidance is an understatement. I only hope that this book stands as some small testament to their abilities as teachers and friends.

The second group to whom I dedicate this book is my family—my husband, Tom Holbrook, and my children, Olivia and Clayton. Being married to a political scientist pays enormous benefits when you are working on a project like this. Tom has been endlessly supportive, both personally and professionally. He has read every draft of this manuscript, has made extensive comments, both stylistic and substantive, and has served as my chief technical adviser. This is a much better book because of his help. He also makes my personal life happier than I could have imagined. Olivia and Clayton, although not involved directly in the production of this manuscript, have contributed every day in the love and joy they bring to my life. With thanks and love, I dedicate this to them.

1

Voters and Women Candidates

Introduction

In a 1999 survey of the political and social attitudes of Americans, 92 percent of those interviewed said they would vote for a qualified woman candidate nominated by their party for president.[1] Yet in October of 1999, fully a year before the 2000 presidential election, Elizabeth Dole ended her quest for the Republican party's nomination amid disappointing efforts at fund-raising and "grumbling at Republican events that it's not a 'woman's place' to run for president."[2] In 2002, incumbent Representative Connie Morella (R-MD) was running in the most competitive election she had faced since being elected to the U.S. House of Representatives in 1986. After redistricting in 2000, her district became more Democratic, giving her Democratic opponent a significant advantage. Morella's strategy for overcoming this partisan disadvantage? She turned to the women voters in her district with an aggressive media campaign to demonstrate her commitment to the issues of importance to them. Whereas women in the United States, and in Morella's district, are more likely to be Democrats than Republicans, Morella was banking on a sense of gender identity and gender representation to pull women voters in her direction. In the end, this strategy failed to pay off for her, and Morella lost her reelection bid. According to one analyst, this was not a complete surprise because "women voters have not been as eager to vote for women candidates as they have in the past."[3]

Electing women to office takes two things: women who will stand as candidates, and voters who will vote for them. Recent work in political science has greatly expanded our understanding of the first part of the equation—when and why women run for office. But there has been comparatively little work that focuses on the second part—whether, when, and why people support women candidates with their vote. This work is intended to address this second issue. Who votes for women candidates? Why do they do so? How does the public evaluate these women? Asking these questions is important because there still seems to be a disconnect between what voters say and what they do regarding women candidates in American politics. Survey data indicate high levels of support for women candidates in the abstract. Yet anecdotal evidence of lingering public uneasiness with women in the political arena abounds, and experimental research suggests that bias against women candidates still exists.[4]

Despite an ever-increasing number of women candidates, there are limits on what we know about them and their relationship to the public because of very real limits on the data and methods we employ to seek answers to our questions about them. If we are to develop a more complete understanding of the place of women candidates in American politics, and of the importance (or lack thereof) of candidate sex in American elections, we need a more systematic analysis of how candidate sex operates in the electoral environment of the real world.

One of the major reasons for the lack of information on public support for women candidates is that, until recently, the number of women candidates in American politics was small, so there were too few cases to study systematically. For example, as recently as 1970, the number of women who ran for congressional or statewide office was 26. By the election of 2002, that number had increased to 232.[5] The increasing number of women candidates means that more and more voters are presented with the option of choosing a woman candidate. This increase in the number of people being faced with a woman candidate provides an excellent opportunity to examine the influence of candidate sex on voters in the real world. It is no longer necessary to rely exclusively on survey data of hypothetical election situations in which people might feel pressure to appear fair and open-minded by voicing support for women candidates, or in which it is easy to *say* that you would vote for a woman because you really don't have to make that choice. Instead, we can examine the voting decisions of people faced with the choice of a woman candidate versus a male candidate and attempt to uncover the role candidate sex might have played in their decision. To that end, this research will address a number of questions about women candidates and the impact of candidate sex on voters' attitudes and behaviors.

First, we want to consider how people think about women candidates. Do voters evaluate women candidates differently than they do men? Do they have as much information, or perhaps different kinds of information, about women candidates? What do voters expect women candidates to be like politically with regard to issues and political ideology? Second, we want to examine voting behavior. In terms of voting behavior generally, we know that such considerations as party identification and candidate incumbency are among the largest influences on a person's vote choice.[6] One of the major questions to ask in this study, then, is how candidate sex can influence vote choice relative to other central influences. Can the presence of a woman candidate overwhelm traditional voting considerations, or do voters behave in the usual way even when a woman candidate is present? To determine answers to these questions, we must examine who votes for women candidates. Are the people who vote for women candidates different from those who choose to vote for men? Are any differences in the characteristics of voters who choose women consistent over time? Are issues important to people's vote choice when a woman candidate is involved? Are the decisions to vote for women candidates influenced by the environment of the election itself?

The rest of this chapter will present an overview of the current state of knowledge about how the public, and in particular, voters, respond to women candidates. This overview will no doubt demonstrate that although we have learned much, there are still many questions about how and when candidate sex is a relevant aspect of elections in American politics.

The Potential Role of Candidate Sex in Elections

A book dedicated to examining the relationship between women candidates and voters makes an assumption that candidate sex matters to public attitudes and behaviors. As we will see, there is reason to make this assumption, but the evidence for when and how candidate sex influences these things is somewhat unclear. Perhaps the best place to start is by discussing why we assume candidate sex has an impact on elections.

Candidate sex becomes a meaningful consideration in American elections because of the central importance of information. Voters need some basic amount of information about candidates and issues if they are to make anything other than a random vote choice. But, as much work on American politics has demonstrated, acquiring information about politics is not often at the top of most citizens' "to do" lists.[7] For many people, time invested in following politics and working to obtain the needed information is time taken away from more central concerns like family, work, and recreation. In such a situation, voters can adopt one of two strategies: They can determine that the information-gathering exercise is not worth their time and effort and opt out of voting, or they can work to find ways to make acquiring information easier and less costly. This second approach is the one many American voters pursue.

Beginning with the work of Anthony Downs in the 1950s, political scientists have examined the ways in which voters work to obtain needed information at a relatively low cost to themselves.[8] We talk about voters using "shortcuts" to developing information. The classic example of this process is political party identification. If they know nothing else, the average voter can fairly easily learn the party identification of a candidate through the media, through printed or electronic campaign advertising, or even by viewing it on the ballot at election time. Once a candidate's party identification is known, an individual can make inferences about that candidate based on the individual's understanding of the policies, positions, and actions of other members of that political party, namely, perhaps, that Democratic candidates are considered more liberal than Republican candidates. A voter who considers herself a Democrat can reasonably assume that she will agree more with the positions and actions of a Democratic candidate than a Republican one and can make a vote choice based on this information with some measure of surety.

According to Samuel Popkin, the public can infer two types of information about candidates from the sorts of information shortcuts described above: issue position and general competence. Issue position is certainly important to many voters. Where a candidate stands on an issue can be an important consideration in determining for whom to vote.[9] In utilizing shortcuts, voters often assume that a Republican candidate's position on tax cuts is in line with the Republican party's position, which will generally be more conservative than the Democratic party's position. However, given that some voters do not have well-developed issue positions of their own, policy position may not be a central concern for all voters. Instead, some may be more concerned with general ideas about candidate competence. Will a candidate be able to do the job? Does the candidate possess the right skills and abilities to be effective in office? Will the candidate get things done?

While most work on information shortcuts has focused on party identification, there are other candidate cues that can give voters important information. Among the most central of these are demographic characteristics, such as sex, race, ethnicity, and religion, with the most obvious being sex and race.[10] With regard to women candidates, voters who have any visual contact with the candidate or, in most cases, hear or see her name will be able to discern her sex. One question then in considering how voters develop a response to candidates is whether demographic cues such as sex are relevant to them. Based on past research in political science and psychology, the answer is a resounding "yes."[11] However, when voters view a candidate's sex, it is not simply whether that candidate is male or female that stimulates the impressions they draw. Instead, the cue offered by candidate sex works in concert with prior beliefs that people have about that cue (here, the general category "women"), which drives their evaluation.[12]

Then we must also consider the differences between the terms *sex* and *gender*. While these terms are often used interchangeably, I would argue that doing so conflates two different considerations. While sex refers to the biological distinctions between female and male, gender is a more complex and socially constructed reference to the categories "feminine" and "masculine." Gender involves ideas about the behaviors, roles, and activities that are considered feminine and masculine as well as beliefs about which people (women or men) appropriately occupy those spaces. But sex and gender, although not mutually exclusive, are also not perfectly aligned. People, both female and male, possess feminine or masculine characteristics or both at the same time. We must keep in mind, then, that what voters see when looking at a woman candidate is her sex, but what they think about her might be based on ideas about gender. So the information that people take when they consider a candidate's sex is very likely filtered through a set of attitudes that they hold, which may or may not lead them to perceive the information "correctly."

The Important Role of Stereotypes

The notion of gender stereotypes is key to the literature on the impact of candidate sex on the attitudes and behaviors of voters. Gender stereotypes involve ideas, shaped by gender considerations, about what is proper or expected from women and men. Over the course of a lifetime of experiences, people develop a set of expectations about how women think and behave, both as women and as they are different from men. These same stereotypes applied to family, workplace, and social interactions are often transmitted to the political world. Indeed, there is significant evidence to suggest that voters look at women candidates and women officeholders from a gendered perspective, ascribing certain stereotyped issue position competencies and personality characteristics to them. These evaluations of women in politics tend to be of two types, known as *gender-trait* stereotypes and *gender-belief* stereotypes.[13] The former refers to a candidate's gender-linked personality traits, whereas the latter deals with gender-linked positions on policy issues.

●   ●   ●

In terms of gender-linked personality traits, women candidates and officeholders are generally viewed as more compassionate and honest than men, warmer and more expressive, and better able to deal with constituents such as citizens groups than men. Men, on the other hand, are viewed as more competent, more decisive, stronger leaders, and more able to handle a crisis.[14] Some work finds that women are evaluated as possessing more feminine traits and skills even when they send a more "masculine" message to the public.[15] Related to this idea is the greater value the public places on the personality traits viewed as "male." Several studies have found that people associate the stereotyped masculine traits such as experience, leadership, and competence as more important in politics than the feminine traits of honesty, warmth, and compassion, particularly as the level of elected office being considered rises from the local to the national level.[16]

Evaluations of women candidates and officeholders generally conform to stereotyped thinking about issue positions as well. Women are assumed to be more interested in, and more effective in dealing with, such issues as child care, poverty, education, health care, women's issues, and the environment than are men, whereas men are thought to be more competent at dealing with economic development, the military, trade, taxes, and agriculture.[17] In terms of political ideology, numerous studies find that women are perceived as more liberal than men and that they are usually perceived as more liberal *than they actually are*, based on objective measures of ideology.[18]

Although the presence of significant gender stereotypes in the minds of voters is evidence itself of the impact of candidate sex on political attitudes, it is understanding the potential impact of these stereotypes on voting behavior that is particularly important. The bottom line for any candidate is the number of votes he or she receives from the public. If voters hold stereotyped attitudes about the abilities and issue positions of women candidates, these judgments may lead certain voters to choose to support or to reject a woman candidate, which could have an impact on the electoral bottom line. In fact, there is some evidence to suggest that voters may use their stereotyped impressions of candidates when formulating a vote choice. But the evidence of the impact of these stereotypes is mixed, with some work demonstrating that voters might be less likely to vote for women whereas other work suggests that stereotypes can actually pull voters toward women candidates. This lack of a consistent impact demonstrates the complex considerations of candidate sex in elections.

Several research works have sought to examine the link between stereotypes of women and men candidates and vote choice. One such work found that women candidates were viewed as more interested in honest government than were men candidates and that voters for whom government ethics was a primary issue concern were more likely to choose women candidates than were other respondents.[19] Other work points to the important role of political party as a mediating influence on the impact of stereotypes. For example, one study demonstrates that voter stereotypes may actually help Republican women candidates among Democratic and Independent voters. Voters were more likely to evaluate Republican women candidates as more moderate than Republican men and expressed a greater willingness to vote for them.

Conversely, however, Republicans were *less* likely to choose the Republican women candidates for exactly the same reason: They perceived Republican women as more moderate than Republican men, too moderate for their tastes.[20] Confirming these findings is research that shows that stereotyped thinking about women candidates increased the perceived ideological distance between Democratic women candidates and voters, which led to a 6 percentage point drop in support for these women. On the other hand, stereotypes decreased the distance between Republican women candidates and voters, actually increasing their vote support by 3–4 percentage points.[21] Finally, recent research on stereotypes presents a way of thinking about the tendency of stereotypes to influence support for women candidates both positively and negatively. Here the evidence suggests that people possess a "baseline preference" to support either a woman or a man candidate. This baseline preference is shaped by people's stereotypes about issue competence and personality traits of women and men. Vote choice, then, is based on a person's baseline preference and whether there is a candidate of the preferred sex in the election. Indeed, more than 50 percent of the respondents in a recent survey expressed a baseline preference for candidates of a particular sex.[22] Clearly, these findings suggest a real potential for stereotypes to influence vote choice and, ultimately, a woman candidate's chance of electoral success.

Evidence of the Impact of Candidate Sex

This book suggests that candidate sex is relevant in elections because it transmits information to voters, who then take in this information and use it to shape their candidate evaluations and vote choices. The research on stereotypes confirms that people come to a particular set of conclusions or evaluations about candidates when those candidates are women. But beyond its impact on stereotyped evaluations, does candidate sex influence other aspects of the public's political attitudes and behaviors?

Because the number of women candidates for office in the United States has increased since the 1970s, and particularly since 1990, researchers have been able to examine more closely whether candidate sex is relevant in any way to the attitudes and behaviors of the mass public. Take, for example, the congressional elections of 1992, the much-heralded "Year of the Woman." Several studies demonstrate that a focus on the sex of women candidates (and gender-related issues) in that election had an impact on the voters and the public at large. For example, the presence of women candidates in 1992 was significantly associated with higher levels of political involvement, political efficacy, and media use by both women and men, with particularly strong effects for women.[23] Others have found that

the presence of women Senate candidates that year increased the psychological engagement of women in the election and that living in a state or
district in which a woman was running for governor or Congress boosted
the media attentiveness and electoral activities of women.[24] With respect
to voting, analysis of voting patterns demonstrates that the determinants
of voter support for women candidates for Congress in 1992 were unique,
with voters displaying different decision-making processes in voting for
women that year than in voting for men, even controlling for party differences.[25] Women candidates in 1992 even had an impact on elections by
changing the behaviors of their male opponents![26]

Clearly, the results of these studies indicate that an election dynamic
that includes women candidates can have a particular impact on the public, especially among women voters. Yet part of the dilemma surrounding
our limited understanding of how this gender dynamic operates is
demonstrated by these same works. For all of the influence that the presence of women candidates seemed to have on voter attitudes and behaviors in 1992, much of the same literature fails to find a similar influence
for candidate sex in either prior or subsequent elections. The presence of
women Senate candidates in 1992 increased psychological engagement in
politics for women, but women Senate candidates in 1990 did not produce
the same effect.[27] Susan Hansen finds that women candidates for Congress
increased efficacy and political engagement of both women and men in
1992, but not at all in 1990 or 1994.[28] In examining vote choice, Kathleen
Dolan finds that candidate sex was important to the public in voting for
women candidates for the U.S. House of Representatives in 1992, but she
saw no evidence of an impact for candidate sex in either 1994 or 1996.[29]
Other works that find an impact for candidate sex focus exclusively on
1992, limiting our ability to generalize beyond that year.[30]

What this research suggests is that there is a potential for candidate sex
to have an impact on elections, but that this impact is not realized in all
elections. For some reason, candidate sex seems to matter more in some
election years or situations than in others. If, as was suggested previously,
candidate sex is a piece of information communicated to voters, the influence of that information may be affected by the circumstances of a particular election. This is another consideration regarding candidate sex that
this book will examine.

As the discussion outlined above suggests, the role of sex and gender in American elections is a complex one that researchers don't yet fully understand. Many scholars have found that the public holds stereotyped evaluations of women candidates and that these stereotypes can have an impact on vote choice. Sometimes these stereotypes can hurt women candidates, and sometimes they can provide women candidates with an advantage. Still other work demonstrates that candidate sex doesn't have a particular impact on voters or vote choice. One of the major goals of this book, then, is to help clarify these issues and uncover if, when, and how candidate sex and gender issues matter in elections

Why Might People Vote for Women Candidates?

Implicit in any study of voting for women candidates is the idea that their sex matters, that voters are choosing a *woman* candidate, as opposed to choosing a candidate without any consideration of his or her sex. Of course, voting for a woman candidate can certainly be an "accidental" act: A voter may choose a candidate who shares his or her political party or policy position on an important issue without the candidate's sex or gender-related issues coming into play. Indeed, we know from countless works that political party is the strongest predictor of vote choice at every level of elected office. But there is research suggesting that voters often do seek out particular types of candidates, candidates with certain characteristics (for example, sex, race, age) for a host of reasons. Most of those reasons focus on questions of representation.

Hanna Pitkin, in her classic work, discusses representation as a complex concept with more than one meaning.[31] She describes two approaches voters take in terms of political representation—when a voter chooses a candidate to hold some decision-making office. First, representation can be *descriptive*, whereby a representative "stands for" others based on a "resemblance or reflection" between them.[32] Second, representation can involve activity, acting on behalf of others. This form of representation is known as *substantive* representation. Both forms of representation are relevant for the study of voting for women candidates. Despite the gains made by women elected officials in the contemporary period, women are still largely "absent" from the halls of government. Their underrepresentation at all levels of office is obvious and undeniable. Thought of this way, descriptive representation occurs when voters choose women candidates because they see the absence of women in office and seek to change that status quo. Elected women officials then serve the function of "standing for" women in the larger society in a very literal way that male representatives cannot.

In a recent essay on the value of descriptive representation for such underrepresented groups as women and racial minorities, Jane Mansbridge argues that descriptive representation is important to our political system for a number of reasons.[33] First, the presence of more officeholders from underrepresented groups demonstrates to the public that members of these groups have "the ability to rule" and that our polity can overcome past discriminatory practices. She also suggests that increased representation of women and minorities can increase communication between government and members of these groups who may mistrust unrepresentative governments and increase the quality of policy deliberations through the contributions of those whose voices had previously been excluded.

Although important, descriptive representation by women candidates and officeholders is not necessarily sufficient as an explanation for why people vote for women candidates. We do not elect government officials merely to stand (or sit) in office and reflect who we are demographically. Instead, we expect them to govern, to act in our best interests. So people who choose women candidates may also do so because they want these women to pursue a particular set of policies once in office. Part of the argument in favor of electing women to achieve substantive representation is the idea that women candidates are better suited than men to address concerns of particular interest to women in the larger society. Given the degree to which the public sees the abilities of women and men candidates in gender-stereotyped ways, we should not be surprised if many people assume that women candidates would be more effective in dealing with issues and policies of concern to women.

From a theoretical perspective, there are clear reasons why voters may choose to cast a vote for a woman candidate. The question that remains is whether or not voting for women candidates helps to achieve these representational goals. Current research on these questions points to an affirmative answer. Taking descriptive representation first, it probably makes more sense that, whereas some men might choose a woman candidate because they recognize the degree to which women are underrepresented in elected office, women voters are more likely to be seeking descriptive representation by voting for women candidates. Indeed, there is significant evidence that women voters often choose women candidates based on a shared sense of identity, or what some researchers call an "affinity effect." The basis for this is a psychological feeling of connection with women, the presence of a gender consciousness.[34] In her work, Cindy Simon Rosenthal finds that women have a stronger preference for same-sex representation than do men. Women are also more likely to vote for a woman candidate than are men and are more apt to see women candidates as sharing their concerns. Among women, the preference for same-sex representation is strongest among older women, those with more feminist attitudes, and those who identify with women as a group. Rosenthal's work is supported by that of Gerald Pomper, who puts forward the idea of the "dependent voter," a person who casts his or her vote based on social group membership and group solidarity rather than on political factors.[35]

Several recent studies have confirmed the idea that women are more likely to vote for women candidates than are men. Posing questions about a hypothetical election race between a woman and a man, Kira Sanbonmatsu demonstrated that women were more likely to have a preference for candidates of a particular sex than were men and were more likely to prefer women, whereas men had no real identifiable sense of gender affinity at work when choosing candidates.[36] This may well be because men in the United States are not in a position of feeling underrepresented in governing bodies and, as a result, do not need to seek out male representation for any particular reason. Women, on the other hand, have a quite different experience. The tendency for women to be more likely than men to choose women candidates is demonstrated in research based both on experiments and hypothetical election races and from surveys of voters from actual elections.[37]

However, in some circumstances, this support is conditioned by other factors, such as race, political party, voter attitudes, or level of office. For example, research indicates that African American women were more likely than African American men to support women candidates, but the authors found no differences among white voters.[38] Others have found that women are more likely to support women candidates when those women run as Democrats, but they are not as supportive of women Republicans.[39] Other researchers suggest that candidate sex is only relevant for voters for whom gender equality issues are particularly important.[40] And other work indicates that this "affinity effect" can vary by level of office. For example, evidence from the 1992 election demonstrated that women were more likely than men to vote for women candidates for the House of Representatives but no more likely to support women Senate candidates.[41] So even though descriptive representation is clearly on the minds of many voters when faced with the choice of a woman candidate, other considerations important to vote choice can come into play. This points to the complex nature of the influence of candidate sex and gender on U.S. elections.

Research also provides support for the role women candidates play in providing substantive representation on women's issues. As stated above, substantive representation is predicated on the idea that electing more women to office will increase the likelihood that women's interests will be addressed by policymakers because women believe and behave differently from men. Most of the work on whether women officeholders provide substantive representation has focused on women elected to state legislatures and to the U.S. Congress. This research tends to use a comparative analysis of the policy priorities and legislative activities of women and men in these various bodies to examine whether women legislators are more likely than men to hold distinctive policy priorities that center around women's issues.

Defining "women's interests" usually takes two forms. First, there is a set of concerns termed "women's traditional issues," such as education, children and family, and health care. A second categorization addresses "feminist issues," issues that have a differential impact on women's lives, such as abortion, sexual harassment, rape laws, and affirmative action. Much of the evidence on the activities of women and men legislators supports the hypothesis that women legislators do indeed express more interest in issues (of both types) of importance to women and that they spend more of their legislative time and effort advancing these causes.[42] But, as with descriptive representation, there are some caveats to make.

Beginning in the 1970s, research supported the notion of difference between women and men elected officials. One of the earliest works examining the activities of women officer-holders found sex differences among local politicians on women's issues such as abortion, affirmative action, and rape law, but no differences on more general issues, such as transportation or the environment.[43] This, of course, makes sense from the perspective of substantive representation. Women candidates and officeholders are expected to provide different treatment of issues of direct concern to women, but there is no reason to assume sex differences on other non–women's issues. This general pattern of women investing greater efforts on behalf of women's issues has been demonstrated among local level officials, state legislators, and members of the U.S. Congress.[44]

However, at the same time that significant evidence supports the idea that women officials spend more of their time pursuing women's issues than do men, contradictory evidence does exist, requiring us to acknowledge that women don't always or automatically provide substantive representation on women's issues once in office.[45] Beth Reingold's study of legislators in California and Arizona suggests that although women do make a difference in terms of substantive representation on some issues some of the time, there are not large, systematic differences between women and men in these legislatures. She suggests several explanations for this disparity, including the idea that legislators, women or men, are elites who must operate inside a set of institutional, party, and constituent constraints that may limit their ability to behave as they wish all of the time. But she also suggests that clear sex differences on women's issues may not be visible because it may be that no clear definition of what it means to "represent women's interests" exists among women candidates and officeholders.[46]

Indeed, stereotyped assumptions about women elites might expect women candidates to take liberal positions and to voice support for women's issues. But these assumptions take a particular direction (liberal, feminist), and we would not expect more conservative, traditional women to embrace the same issues simply because they are women. From the perspective of substantive representation, then, we have to ask whether there is a "women's interest" that is identifiable and definable. Is there a common set of values or issues that women hold on to that women candidates and officials can act on to meet the needs of women?

Although a woman candidate's sex is demonstrably important for reasons of representation, these issues of representation also point to the complexity involved in our assumptions about women candidates. Most common here is the tendency to link descriptive and substantive representation and to expect both from women elected to office. The evidence indicates that some voters, especially women, prefer women candidates and often choose them to achieve some notion of descriptive representation. But tied closely to this descriptive perspective is the assumption that once more women are elected, they will behave in a particular way that benefits women, providing substantive representation as well. Much of the evidence to date supports this notion. However, other evidence provides mixed support and may cause us to examine more closely who these women are. In fact, at all levels of office in the United States, women candidates and elected officials are more likely to be Democrats than Republicans. It may well be that a definable set of "women's interests" exists among a group of women who are likely to embrace a more liberal set of policies in general. But Republican women, who may be more conservative than their Democratic women counterparts, may see their efforts toward ending abortion or affirmative action or their seeking covenant marriage laws as furthering "women's interests" as well. They simply define a different set of interests as important to women. And so here is the rub: Electing women because they are women will not ensure a particular approach to women's issues. The link between being a woman and acting in a particular way with regard to women's issues is not a guaranteed one.

Perhaps a good recent example of this is former U.S. Representative Helen Chenoweth (R-ID), who served from 1994 to 2000. Representative Chenoweth refused to be addressed as Congresswoman Chenoweth because, as she believed, the position to which she was elected was "Congressman," and she was simply the person holding the office. She saw no reason to modify the traditional job title to accurately reflect her sex. Clearly, a woman who refers to herself as Congressman is not going to spend her legislative career working for what is generally seen as "women's issues." So, while she may have been providing descriptive representation for women of Idaho and the nation, she was not actively working to provide women with substantive representation of their needs. Voters seeking substantive representation from such a candidate on the basis of her sex alone may have been disappointed with the outcome.

Moving Beyond Hypotheticals:
The National Election Study

It should be clear from the preceding discussions that there has been a significant amount of research undertaken by political scientists in efforts to uncover the importance (or lack thereof) of candidate sex in American elections. Yet despite the volume of this research, we must proceed with caution in drawing conclusions because of the way in which much of this research was carried out. Going back to the first studies of the role of candidate sex in the 1970s, much of the work that examined the relationship between women candidates and the public has employed some sort of experiment or quasi-experimental design based on the presentation of hypothetical candidates and election matchups to research samples.[47] This is not to say that these approaches make this work irrelevant to our understanding. Indeed, the use of experiments and quasi-experiments offers the advantage of a controlled environment that is often necessary for isolating the impact of candidate sex on a person's political evaluations. However, we must also acknowledge that the response a survey participant gives when asked to evaluate two hypothetical candidates in a fictitious election may not reveal fully the calculations that person would make when evaluating two candidates in an actual election. Such situations also do not approximate the real political world and the competing influences of political party identification, ideology, or incumbency.

Of course, one of the reasons for this traditional reliance on hypothetical election situations has been the relatively small number of women candidates, which results in a small number of people in the mass public who have actually been faced with a woman candidate. If you want to know what the public thinks about women candidates in a real-world context, you need people who have had the opportunity to evaluate one (or more) and to make a decision to vote for or against her. Until recently, that simply wasn't possible, or at least not possible without tremendous amounts of research money to find and interview these people. But since the early 1990s, as the number of women candidates has increased, researchers have begun to take advantage of these changes and to test their hypotheses about the role of candidate sex in real election situations. One of the primary data sources for doing this is the National Election Study (NES) conducted by the University of Michigan, which constitutes the

primary source of data for this project. The National Election Study interviews a representative sample of Americans every election year, talking
with them both before and after the election in a presidential election year
and conducting postelection interviews in the congressional-only years.[48]
The survey covers a wide range of political, social, and demographic issues, providing a fairly comprehensive picture of the political attitudes
and behaviors of the American public.

One of the substantive areas that the NES examines is how voters evaluate
political candidates. To determine these evaluations, respondents are asked
an extensive series of questions about their feelings toward presidential and
congressional candidates and questions about their vote choice in these
races. These questions give us an invaluable source of information about
how people evaluate women candidates and whether and when voters are
choosing them, exactly the information that has been lacking in previous
examinations of the fortunes of women candidates. When we combine
these data with demographic and issue position information about respondents who were faced with women candidates, we can begin to construct a
series of explanations for how and why people support women candidates.

Although the sample of people included in the NES each year is a representative sample of the U.S. population, respondents are not drawn from
each state, nor are they drawn from each congressional district in a particular state. The result of this method is that the NES does not necessarily
interview people in every district or state in which a woman candidate is
running. As a result, we do not have information on every woman candidate running in a particular year. But for the time period under examination here, 1990 to 2000, 46 percent of the women candidates for Congress
ran in districts or states represented in the NES surveys.[49] Over the ten-
year period, this gives us a substantial sample of people who have been
presented with a woman candidate: 1,093 respondents who were faced
with women candidates for the House and 1,296 respondents who could
choose a woman candidate for the Senate.

Chapter Plans

This book seeks to contribute to our knowledge about the way the public
evaluates women candidates in three ways. First, by employing data from

the growing body of surveys conducted with voters in actual elections, I hope to be able to move beyond the knowledge based on hypotheticals and experiments to determine how real voters perceive real women candidates. Second, I will examine both how voters evaluate women candidates and whether or not they vote for them. Finally, I will move beyond the single election approach of many other works and examine the period during which we have seen a steady increase in the number of women candidates for Congress: 1990 to 2000. To accomplish these goals, the remainder of the book will address several issues. Chapter 2 presents a brief history of women candidates in U.S. elections. It offers a historical view of the public's attitudes toward women in political life and how those attitudes have changed over time. This chapter also addresses the numerous legal and cultural challenges to their candidacies that women have overcome, along with presenting data on the growth of the number of women candidates in American politics and an overview of their participation as candidates at various levels of office (local, statewide, and national).

Chapter 3 begins the examination of how voters evaluate women candidates by considering the public's attitudes toward women candidates, specifically the degree to which people hold gender-stereotyped impressions of women candidates as well as whether women candidates are seen in a positive or negative light. Chapter 4 asks the question "Who Votes for Women in American Elections?" This chapter is the first of two that seek to develop explanations for voter support for women candidates running for Congress. In this chapter, the focus is on determining what type of people are more likely to support women candidates by examining the demographic characteristics of these voters. As I discussed earlier, primary among the relevant demographic variables is voter sex, but past literature has found that other variables such as race, age, education, and religion can significantly shape a person's likelihood of choosing a woman candidate.

In Chapter 5, the analysis moves beyond a demographic explanation to uncover the role that issue positions play in vote choice. Here I test a model that accounts for the influence of issues on vote choice. If the literature on stereotypes indicates that people often see women candidates as having particular issue strengths, we might expect to see people vote for women candidates when they place a high value on issues on which women are seen to be competent (for example, education) and be less likely to vote for them when they see other types of issues as most important (say, military or economic issues). This argument suggests that voters may cast a vote for or against a woman candidate depending on the issue positions they take.

Chapter 6, based on findings from Chapters 4 and 5, advances an argument that voters do not respond to women candidates in one consistent fashion and that the impact of candidate sex can vary significantly from election to election. Returning to the idea that candidate sex acts as a piece of information to voters in the electoral environment, this chapter suggests that the amount of information about women candidates and gender issues can play a key role. Finally, Chapter 7 ties together the various questions raised by this work and the conclusions that can be drawn from the data analysis. In this chapter, I evaluate the explanations for voter support of women candidates in congressional elections and discuss future directions for research.

Notes

1. Newport, Frank, David Moore, and Lydia Saad, "Long Term Gallup Poll Trends: A Portrait of American Public Opinion Through the Century," *Gallup Report*, December 20, 1999.

2. Feldman, Linda, Francine Kiefer, and James Thurman, "Dole's Candidacy Has Historic Impact," *Christian Science Monitor*, October 21, 1999, p. 1.

3. Celinda Lake, quoted in "Tug of War over Women in Maryland's 8th," by Jo Becker and Dan Balz, *The Washington Post*, October 20, 2002, p. 1.

4. Fox, Richard, and Eric R.A.N. Smith, "The Role of Candidate Sex in Voter Decision-Making," *Political Psychology* 19 (1998):405–419.

5. Center for American Women and Politics (CAWP), *Fact Sheet*, "Women Candidates in 2002: Congressional and Statewide Office" (New Brunswick, N.J.: Eagleton Institute of Politics, Rutgers University, 2002).

6. Abramson, Paul, John Aldrich, and David Rohde, *Change and Continuity in the 2000 Elections* (Washington, D.C.: CQ Press, 2002); Jacobson, Gary, *The Politics of Congressional Elections*, 5th ed. (New York: Longman, 2001).

7. Delli Carpini, Michael, and Scott Keeter, *What Americans Know About Politics and Why It Matters* (New Haven: Yale University Press, 1996).

8. Conover, Pamela, and Stanley Feldman, "Candidate Perception in an Ambiguous World," *American Journal of Political Science* 33 (1989):912–939; Downs, Anthony *An Economic Theory of Democracy* (New York: Harper, 1957); Popkin, Samuel, "Information Shortcuts and the Reasoning Voter," in *Information, Participation, and Choice: An Economic Theory*

of Democracy in Perspective, ed. Bernard Grofman (Ann Arbor: University of Michigan, 1993); Rahn, Wendy, "The Role of Partisan Stereotypes in Information Processing about Political Candidates," *American Journal of Political Science* 37 (1993):472–496.

9. Marcus, Gregory, and Philip Converse, "A Dynamic Simultaneous Equation Model of Electoral Choice," *American Political Science Review* 73 (1979):1055–1070; Page, Benjamin, and Richard Brody, "Policy Voting and the Electoral Process: The Vietnam War Issue," *American Political Science Review* 66 (1972):979–995.

10. Popkin, Samuel, *The Reasoning Voter* (Chicago: University of Chicago Press, 1991); Sapiro, Virginia, "If U.S. Senator Baker Were a Woman: An Experimental Study of Candidate Images," *Political Psychology* 3 (1981/82):61–83.

11. McDermott, Monika, "Voting Cues in Low-Information Elections: Candidate Gender as a Social Information Variable in Contemporary United States Elections," *American Journal of Political Science* 41 (1998):270–283.

12. Feldman, Stanley, and Pamela Johnston Conover, "Candidates, Issues, and Voters: The Role of Inference in Political Perception," *Journal of Politics* 45 (1983):810–839.

13. Huddy, Leonie, and Nayda Terkildsen, "Gender Stereotypes and the Perception of Male and Female Candidates," *American Journal of Political Science* 37 (1993a):119–147.

14. Alexander, Deborah, and Kristi Andersen, "Gender as a Factor in the Attribution of Leadership Traits," *Political Research Quarterly* 46 (1993):527–545; Huddy and Terkildsen 1993a; Kahn, Kim, "Does Being Male Help? An Investigation of the Effects of Candidate Gender and Campaign Coverage on Evaluations of U.S. Senate Candidates," *Journal of Politics* 54 (1992):497–517; King, David, and Richard Matland, "Partisanship and the Impact of Candidate Gender in Congressional Elections: Results of an Experiment," paper presented at the Women Transforming Congress conference, Carl Albert Center, University of Oklahoma, 1999; Koch, Jeffrey, "Candidate Gender and Assessments of Senate Candidates," *Social Science Quarterly* 80 (1999):84–96; Leeper, Mark, "The Impact of Prejudice on Female Candidates: An Experimental Look at Voter Inference," *American Politics Quarterly* 19 (1991):248–261.

15. Leeper 1991; Sapiro 1981/82.

16. Huddy, Leonie, and Nayda Terkildsen, "The Consequences of Gender Stereotypes for Women Candidates at Different Levels and Types of Offices," *Political Research Quarterly* 46 (1993b):503–525; Rosenwasser, Shirley, and Norma Dean, "Gender Role and Political Office: Effects of Perceived Masculinity/Femininity of Candidate and Political Office," *Psychology of Women Quarterly* 13 (1989):77–85.

17. Alexander and Andersen 1993; Brown, Clyde, Neil Heighberger, and Peter Shocket, "Gender-Based Differences in Perceptions of Male and Female City Council Candidates," *Women and Politics* 13 (1993):1–17; Huddy and Terkildsen 1993a; Koch 1999; Rosenwasser and Dean 1989.

18. Koch, Jeffrey, "Do Citizens Apply Gender Stereotypes to Infer Candidates' Ideological Orientations?" *Journal of Politics* 62 (2000):414–429; Koch, Jeffrey, "Gender Stereotypes and Citizens' Impression of House Candidates Ideological Orientations," *American Journal of Political Science* 46 (2002):453–462; McDermott, Monika, "Race and Gender Cues in Low-Information Elections," *Political Research Quarterly* 51 (1997):895–918.

19. McDermott 1998.

20. King and Matland 1999.

21. Koch 2000; Koch 2002.

22. Sanbonmatsu, Kira, "Gender Stereotypes and Vote Choice," *American Journal of Political Science* 46 (2002):20–34.

23. Hansen, Susan, "Talking About Politics: Gender and Contextual Effects on Political Proselytizing," *Journal of Politics* 59 (1997):73–103.

24. Koch, Jeffrey, "Candidate Gender and Women's Psychological Engagement in Politics," *American Politics Quarterly* 25 (1997):118–133; Sapiro, Virginia, and Pamela Johnston Conover, "The Variable Gender Basis of Electoral Politics: Gender and Context in the 1992 US Election," *British Journal of Political Science* 27 (1997):523.

25. Dolan, Kathleen, "Voting for Women in the 'Year of the Woman,'" *American Journal of Political Science* 42 (1998):272–293.

26. Fox, Richard, *Gender Dynamics in Congressional Elections* (Thousand Oaks, Calif.: Sage Publications, 1997).

27. Koch 1997.

28. Hansen 1997.

29. Dolan, Kathleen, "Electoral Context, Issues, and Voting for Women in the 1990s," *Women and Politics* 23 (2001):21–36.

30. Sapiro and Conover 1997.

31. Pitkin, Hanna, *The Concept of Representation* (Berkeley: University of California Press, 1972).

32. Pitkin 1972, p. 61.

33. Mansbridge, Jane, "Should Blacks Represent Blacks and Women Represent Women? A Contingent 'Yes,'" *Journal of Politics* 61 (1999):628–657.

34. Rosenthal, Cindy Simon, "The Role of Gender in Descriptive Representation," *Political Research Quarterly* 48 (1995):599–611.

35. Pomper, Gerald, *Voters' Choice: Varieties of American Electoral Behavior* (New York: Dodd, Mead, 1975).

36. Sanbonmatsu 2002.

37. Cook, Elizabeth, "Voter Responses to Women Senate Candidates," in *The Year of the Woman: Myths and Realities,* eds. Elizabeth Adell Cook, Sue Thomas, and Clyde Wilcox (Boulder: Westview Press, 1994); Dolan, Kathleen, "Gender Differences in Support for Women Candidates: Is There a Glass Ceiling in American Politics?" *Women and Politics* 17 (1997):27–41; Dolan 1998; Ekstrand, Laurie, and William Eckert, "The Impact of Candidate's Sex on Voter Choice," *Western Political Quarterly* 34 (1981):78–87; Hershey, Marjorie, "The Politics of Androgyny: Sex Roles and Attitudes Toward Women in Politics," *American Politics Quarterly* 3 (1977):261–287; Lewis, Carolyn, "Are Women for Women? Feminist and Traditional Values in the Female Electorate," *Women and Politics* 20 (1999):1–28; Paolino, Phillip, "Group-Salient Issues and Group Representation: Support for Women Candidates in the 1992 Senate Elections," *American Journal of Political Science* 39 (1995):294–313; Plutzer, Eric, and John Zipp, "Identity Politics, Partisanship, and Voting

for Women Candidates," *Public Opinion Quarterly* 60 (1996):30–57; Seltzer, Richard, Jody Newman, and Melissa Leighton, *Sex as a Political Variable: Women as Candidates and Voters in U.S. Elections* (Boulder: Lynne Rienner, 1997); Sigelman, Lee, and Carol Sigelman, "Sexism, Racism, and Ageism in Voting Behavior: An Experimental Analysis," *Social Psychology Quarterly* 45 (1982):263–269; Sigelman, Lee, and Susan Welch, "Race, Gender, and Opinion Toward Black and Female Candidates," *Public Opinion Quarterly* 48 (1984):467–475; Zipp, John, and Eric Plutzer, "Gender Differences in Voting for Female Candidates: Evidence from the 1982 Election," *Public Opinion Quarterly* 49 (1982):179–197.

38. Sigelman and Welch 1984.

39. Cook 1994; King and Matland 1999; Seltzer, Newman, and Leighton 1997.

40. Thompson, Seth, and Janie Steckenrider, "The Relative Irrelevance of Candidate Sex," *Women and Politics* 17 (1997):71–92.

41. Dolan 1998.

42. Thomas, Sue, *How Women Legislate* (New York: Oxford University Press, 1994); Welch, Susan, "Are Women More Liberal Than Men in the U. S. Congress?" *Legislative Studies Quarterly* 10 (1985):125–134.

43. Mezey, Susan Gluck, "Support for Women's Rights Policy: An Analysis of Local Politicians," *American Politics Quarterly* 6 (1978):485–497.

44. Boles, Janet, "Advancing the Women's Agenda Within Local Legislatures: The Role of Female Elected Officials," in *Gender and Policymaking: Studies of Women in Office*, ed. Debra Dodson (New Brunswick, N.J.: Center for American Women and Politics, 1991); Bratton, Kathleen, and Kerry Haynie, "Agenda-Setting and Legislative Success in State Legislatures: The Effects of Gender and Race," *Journal of Politics* 61 (1999):658–679; Burrell, Barbara, *A Woman's Place Is in the House: Campaigning for Congress in the Feminist Era* (Ann Arbor: University of Michigan Press, 1994); Dodson, Debra, "Representing Women's Interests in the U.S. House of Representatives," in *Women and Elective Office: Past, Present, and Future*, eds. Sue Thomas and Clyde Wilcox (New York: Oxford University Press, 1998); Saint-Germain, Michelle, "Does Their Difference Make a Difference? The Impact of Women on Public Policy in the Arizona Legislature," *Social Science Quarterly* 70 (1989):956–968; Swers, Michele, *The Difference Women Make: The Policy Impact of Women in Congress* (Chicago: University of Chicago Press, 2002); Thomas, Sue, and Susan Welch, "The Impact of Gender on Activities and Priorities of State Legislators," *Western Political Quarterly* 44 (1991):445–456.

45. Barnello, Michelle, "Gender and Roll Call Voting in the New York State Assembly," *Women and Politics* 20 (1999):77–94.

46. Reingold, Beth, *Representing Women: Sex, Gender and Legislative Behavior in Arizona and California* (Chapel Hill: University of North Carolina Press, 2000).

47. Adams, William, "Candidate Characteristics, Office of Election, and Voter Responses," *Experimental Study of Politics* 4 (1975):76–88; Dolan 1997; Ekstrand and Eckert 1981; Fox and Smith 1998; Hershey 1977; Huddy and Terkildsen 1993a; Huddy and Terkildsen 1993b; Kahn 1992; King and Matland 1999; Leeper 1991; McDermott 1997; Riggle, Ellen, Penny Miller, Todd G. Shields, and Mitzi Johnson, "Gender Stereotypes and Decision

Context in the Evaluation of Political Candidates," *Women and Politics* 17 (1997):69–88; Rosenwasser and Dean 1989; Sanbonmatsu 2002; Sapiro 1981/82; Sigelman and Sigelman 1982; Thompson and Streckenrider 1997.

48. The number of people interviewed generally ranges from 1,500–2,400, depending on the year.

49. See Appendix A for complete information about the NES survey.

2

A Brief History of
Women in U.S. Elections

··

"Women do the lickin' and stickin' while men plan the strategy."

—Moon Landrieu, Mayor of New Orleans

"The only time to run a woman is when things look so bad that your only chance is to do something dramatic."

—John Bailey, Democratic National Committee Chair

THE TWO FAMOUS POLITICAL MEN quoted above offer a concise sense of the attitude toward women in political life in the United States for much of the twentieth century. Whether in their roles in political parties or as candidates for election, women have largely been relegated to the sidelines and the support positions. Landrieu's quote conjures up images of women performing their stereotypical support functions, doing the "dirty work" so that others can "get things done." Bailey's words evoke the selfless, sacrificing nature women are thought to possess. And even though these quotes reflect a somewhat different time in American political history, the challenges that face women today are still shaped, to some degree, by the same forces. Attitudes toward women in politics have undergone an evolution that is not complete at the beginning of the twenty-first century. Although women are currently represented in political life to a greater degree than ever before, parity is still a long way off.

Sentiments about women in a political capacity are, of course, shaped by long-standing cultural assumptions about the roles women are expected to fulfill. Liberal political thought divides the world into the public and private realms. Men, the thinking goes, are characterized as reasoned and rational, possessing intellect that makes them best suited for the public realm of business, political, and economic life. Women, on the other hand, are driven by intuition, emotion, and a need to nurture, placing them most appropriately in the private world, the center of home and family. For women, this dichotomy stresses the roles of wife, mother, homemaker, and caregiver. For the average woman, political activity was thought to be unnecessary because she would likely have a father or husband to act on behalf of her interests. Beyond public activity being seen as unnecessary for women, it was considered inappropriate and dangerous. Women did not have the right temperament or ability to make the important civic decisions required of those who took part in public life.

For much of U.S. history, women were explicitly denied a political role. Yet even when legal rights were granted to them, women's participation was limited by social and cultural attitudes. In fact, the story of the political life of American women in the twentieth century is more about these informal norms and attitudes than it is about formal legal restrictions. Women have had the right to vote nationwide since 1920, even earlier in a few states, and the right to run for office in every state since the 1940s. But women's realistic opportunities to enter political life are more contemporary. This chapter will explore the evolution of the informal norms and attitudes about women and politics that still shape women's possibilities for success.

A History of Women Candidates in the U.S.

From the Private to the Public—
Women's Entrance into the Political World

In the United States, we often think about 1920 and the granting of woman suffrage as the starting point of much of women's political history. However, despite a system that presented women with both formal and informal barriers to their participation, some women were active in politics, working in social movements, with the political parties, and even holding office, all before women had the right to vote.

The most significant informal barrier to women's entrance into politics was a way of thinking about the world that separated life into public and private arenas, assigning men to the public realm and women to the private. As had been the practice in Europe, it was a given that women in the New World would have no role in political life. They were thought to possess neither the intelligence, the education, nor the temperament to deal with "such an arduous task as politics."[1] The assumption that women rightly belonged in the private world of home and family was so strongly ingrained in people during the colonial time that only one colony had actually bothered to create a statute banning women from voting. And, in a time when women exercising the vote was considered ludicrous, the idea of their holding office was unimaginable. Even an advocate for women's political voice such as Abigail Adams could not envision a political world in which women held power: "Governments of States and kingdoms, tho' God knows how badly enough managed, I am willing should be solely administered by the lords of creation. I should only contend for Domestic government, and think that best administered by the female."[2]

The social values that kept women out of politics at the beginning of our history continued to shape women's activities when they began to make tentative steps into that world. As the 1800s began, some women began to become active in partisan politics, although their activities have been described as "ornamental," with women sewing banners, organizing picnics, and cheering at party rallies. This beginning was seen by some people as acceptable because women's activities were still limited to the sorts of social and organizational tasks at which women were thought to excel. However, even this level of political involvement was not without controversy. Indeed, one anonymous author was quoted as objecting to women who "under that wild infatuation of party enthusiasm, . . . forsook their home paths and appeared in public" in party activities.[3]

The Civil War brought a second expansion of women's activity in the public world through their work in various social causes, particularly the abolition and temperance movements. Women in these organizations took on public roles largely unheard of for women before this point: speaking at public meetings, traveling to spread their beliefs, and writing for pamphlets and newspapers. As with the support roles they played in party organizations, women's involvement in abolition and temperance issues was seen as an extension of their compassionate natures and their concern over the quality of family life. Their assumed "moral authority" brought a sense of legitimacy to the movements in which they took part. Abolitionist Henry Ward Beecher, brother of Harriet Beecher Stowe, wrote that government "needed improvement," as men often resorted to "force, passion, and fraud" in conducting political affairs and that women, with their superior moral nature, would help reform government.[4] Although there were still vocal critics of women's entry into public life, these sorts of activities set a precedent for women's activities that continued forward.

The debate over woman suffrage, which began after the Civil War and continued until the passage of the 19th amendment (and beyond), was clearly one that tested society's beliefs about what was appropriate social and political activity for women. The notion that women's proper place was in the home was a very strong component of the argument against granting women the vote. Concerns were raised about disturbing the "natural roles" that God had ordained for women and men, about the potential for the corruption of women and the destruction of family life, and about expanding the franchise to admit people (women) largely uneducated about, or uninterested in, political issues. Those opposed to suffrage for women appealed to public attitudes about women's place, with a good measure of success. However, once a door is opened, it is difficult to close, and women, who had begun to take some tentative steps into politics, continued to push against the social and cultural attitudes that would confine them to the home.

Early Women in Elected Office—Before Suffrage

Whereas the Revolutionary and Civil War eras saw periods in which women began a slow integration into partisan politics and social movements, the roots of women's experiences as candidates and officeholders in are in the post–Civil War era. In 1866, in order to test the waters, suffrage activist Elizabeth Cady Stanton became the first woman to run for the U.S. Congress when she wrote a public letter announcing her candidacy. She received 24 votes.[5] In 1872, Victoria Woodhull founded the Equal Rights Party, which made her its nominee for president. In 1888, the Equal Rights party nominated Belva Lockwood for president. Around the country, other women began running for office, either as candidates of the Equal Rights Party (such as Linda Gilbert, who ran for governor of New York in 1888) or as Independents (as when Eliza Garner became the first woman candidate in South Carolina in 1888 when she ran for county commissioner). But the greatest activity as women became office-seekers occurred in the western states and territories.

Before women throughout the country were granted suffrage under the 19th Amendment, some states and territories had given women residents the right to vote. Some granted full suffrage, whereas others gave women the vote in municipal elections or on questions of taxation or gave them "school suffrage," the right to vote in elections for school administration officials, such as school board or education commissioner. In these areas, the idea of women as candidates was a bit less foreign than it was in other areas of the country, although female political activity still conformed to general stereotypes about women's capabilities. Kansas provides a good example of this early entry by women candidates. In 1887, an all-female town council was elected in the town of Syracuse and, in 1888, a female mayor and town council were elected in Okaloosa. Both of these so-called "petticoat governments" were reform movements undertaken by women seeking to clean up the corrupt governments run by men. However, once they had enacted reforms, these women generally left government, returning to the "appropriate" sphere of home and family. Another commonality was that women who ran for office during this early period tended to run for school boards or school commissioner. Women, because of their responsibility in educating their children, were seen as having a particular expertise in this area, which helped to overcome public concern about women in the political world.

Third parties tended to be more hospitable to women candidates than the Democratic and Republican parties. In 1894 and after, the Populist party, strong in the southern and western parts of the country, ran women for several offices, including attorney general, state school superintendent, and state legislator in Montana, North Dakota, and Colorado. Indeed, fielding women candidates was thought to be a smart strategic move on the part of third parties because support from female voters could help them win office.[6] This strategy was not lost on the two major parties, who began to back women candidates on occasion. However, support for women candidates was not universal. Concerns were raised that women who entered the political arena risked ruining their femininity and, more to the point, displaced men in office and party politics. As one observer who predicted defeat for Kate Galpin, candidate for school superintendent in Los Angeles, said, "voters believe in women in homes, not in politics."[7]

Women's greatest integration into politics, though still generally limited to education offices and lower-level local positions that did not pay a salary, took place in the first four states to grant women full suffrage: Wyoming, Utah, Colorado, and Idaho. In 1896, Martha Hughes Cannon, a doctor and women's suffrage activist from Salt Lake County, became the first woman elected to a U.S. state legislature when she won a seat in Utah's state senate. Ironically, one of the several candidates she defeated in the at-large election was her husband, Angus.[8] After 1898, dozens of women were elected as state legislators, county treasurers, superintendents of schools, county clerks, and mayors in these states. And many of these women were elected with the votes of women voters. Women's turnout in these four states was strong, with women often making up 40 to 50 percent of the voting population.[9] Another trend that continued as the twentieth century dawned was for women candidates to find support for their office-seeking from third parties. During the 1910s, several women ran for office on Socialist, Prohibition, and Progressive party tickets, particularly in California and Washington.[10]

In what was perhaps the most significant symbolic election before women's suffrage was granted nationally, Jeannette Rankin was elected to the U.S. House of Representatives from Montana in 1916. Before running for Congress, Rankin had worked in philanthropic movements, settlement house work, and suffrage activities. Voicing one of the suffrage movement's themes that women would bring different concerns to politics, she ran for the House, declaring "There are hundreds of men to care for the nation's tariff and foreign policy and irrigation projects. But there isn't a single woman to look after the nation's greatest asset: its children."[11] She campaigned on a platform seeking suffrage for women, prohibition, and occupational safety and health care improvements for women and children. Winning election at age 36, she served one term, being defeated for reelection largely because of her vote in opposition to the United States' entry into World War I. In 1918, she sought the Republican Party's nomination for a U.S. Senate seat from Montana. When she did not receive the nomination, she ran as an Independent, but she lost the election. Rankin ran for the House again, in 1940, serving one term, and she retired without seeking reelection in 1942.[12]

Women Candidates After Suffrage

The ratification of the 19th Amendment, granting universal suffrage to women, was the result of a long-fought, hard-won battle by advocates of women's rights. But suffrage leaders had never made increasing the number of women elected to political office an explicit goal of their campaign. As a result, women's candidacies and office-holding increased after 1920 but at a slow pace, and they were still limited by circumstances and social attitudes.

In fact, one question that had to be addressed after suffrage was whether possessing the right to vote gave women the right to run for office. Immediately after 1920, a vigorous debate took place. Many woman suffrage activists took the position that the right to run for office was a logical extension of the right to vote, a position often supported by political parties seeking to ingratiate themselves with new women voters. Opponents pointed to state laws and constitutions that defined eligibility to hold office based on sex. Interestingly, several states allowed women to hold certain offices, usually school committee members, well before those same states granted suffrage to women. Iowa made women eligible for any office except that of state legislator.[13] But, for the most part, being male was one of the qualifications for holding office. For example, Missouri law required that members of the state legislature "must be a male voter and a voter for two years before the election."[14] After 1920, various challenges to women's candidacies ultimately led to state actions to drop sex-based qualifications for holding all offices, culminating with Oklahoma in 1942.[15]

In the 1920s, women candidates slowly began to seek a broader range of offices at all levels of government than had previously been the case. Local politics remained the domain of activity seen as most appropriate for women. According to Kristi Andersen, local offices such as mayor, school superintendent, county commissioner, or town councilor seemed to many to be a logical extension of women's home management abilities. These offices were also usually part-time, allowing women to serve while not neglecting their primary responsibilities to home and family. Although the data are not readily available, Andersen's analysis demonstrates that as few as five (Alabama) and as many as 137 (Iowa) women were elected to county offices in the states during the period from 1920 to 1933.[16] Even though only a handful of women held statewide elective office, such as secretary of state, treasurer, or state auditor, women candidates were increasingly likely to seek seats in state legislatures. In 1922, a survey of states conducted by *Woman Citizen* found 179 women nominees for state legislative office in 37 states. After that election, 98 women served in state legislatures. By the end of the decade, that number had risen to 149.[17] Of course, although a considerable increase in women's representation, this number must be compared to the approximately 10,000 male state legislators serving at the same time. At the federal level, the 1920s saw nearly 20 women nominated for either the U.S. House or Senate during each election year of the decade. However, the majority of these women congressional candidates were "sacrificial lambs," nominated by the minority party in the district or state that had very little chance of winning the seat.

•   •   •

During the immediate post-suffrage period, there were two major obstacles facing women candidates: reluctant political parties and an often hostile public. In their attempts to overcome these obstacles, many women candidates and their advocates continued to press arguments for women's inclusion in public office based on stereotypes about what was proper activity for women. According to Breckinridge, during the years of debate about suffrage, one prominent argument was that some offices (legislatures, judges in juvenile courts) were most appropriate for women, given their traditional responsibility and interest in issues related to children and the home. Others continued to focus on the presumed differences between women and men, attempting to assure a skeptical public that women officeholders were not "politicians" in the traditional sense. Personal ambition was very rarely a quality embraced by women seeking office in the post-suffrage time. Instead, women candidates were thought to be much more interested in advancing issues than gaining political power.[18] True to their "nature," these women engaged in "municipal housekeeping," extending their organizational habits and purity of morals to the world of politics.[19] By promoting their particular skills as homemakers and focusing on issues on which they were thought to be better versed (social welfare, education, public health, and morals), these women candidates and officeholders sought to reassure an often unfriendly public that their presence in politics would not dramatically alter the world as they knew it.

Women candidates also faced opposition from party organizations. According to Sarah Jane Deutsch, political parties were hesitant to nominate women for offices the party had a realistic chance of winning because this strategy would deny a seat to a man. Part of this hesitation was a result of concern that women did not have "what it took" to win office. One of the themes of the women's suffrage movement was that women, by their pure nature, were above politics and would "clean up" government. But, after arguing that they were above politics, women had to demonstrate that they knew how to play the game.[20] Parties were also often less than enthusiastic about women nominees because they couldn't be sure that women candidates would attract sufficient votes. No "women's bloc" of voters had appeared after suffrage, which is from where the parties expected a woman candidate's support would come. Without this unity of women voters, parties were not often willing to take a chance by nominating women for competitive races. From their perspective, this was not an unreasonable position for parties to take because there was considerable concern among the public about voting for a woman. Although women candidates nominated as sacrificial lambs were probably defeated as much because of the minority position of their party as because of their sex, records indicate that women running as the nominee of the majority party in a district or state often had difficulty attracting votes as well. In such situations, voters would be choosing a male candidate of the other party over a woman candidate of their own party (See, for example, Andersen). Such antiwoman bias is clear in the comments of a male voter to Ruth Hanna McCormick, who ran for Congress from Illinois in 1928. His letter said, in part, "I would not think of voting for a woman for Congressman-At-Large any more than to vote for one of my cows for such a responsible office."[21]

Women's Candidacies in the Contemporary Period

The history of women candidates from the immediate post-suffrage era to the 1970s was one of great similarity—small numbers of women candidates and even smaller numbers of women serving in elected office. Women who ran for elected office during this period had to jump several hurdles, first overcoming the cultural norms that defined politics as a male pursuit[22] and then the skeptical, if not hostile, response from the public, particularly male voters.[23] Given these challenges, low numbers of women seeking office should not be surprising. For example, in 1930 there were 149 women state legislators around the country. Forty years later, in 1970, there were 344 women serving, comprising only 4.5 percent of all state legislators. In 1930, there were 9 women in the U.S. Congress, all in the

House of Representatives. In 1970, there were 11 women, 10 in the House and one in the Senate. These 11 women were elected from the total pool of 26 women candidates for Congress that year.[24] Clearly, for much of the twentieth century, the story of women candidates was a very limited one.

As Table 2.1 indicates, a different pattern in women's candidacies begins to appear after 1970. From 1970 to 2002, the number of women candidates for state legislative office has more than doubled, from 1,125 to 2,345. The number of women congressional candidates jumped from 26 in 1970 to 135 in 2002. Similar patterns of increase can be seen for governor and have been documented for other statewide offices, such as lieutenant governor, attorney general, secretary of state, and state treasurer. Even though women's candidacies still do not reflect their presence in the population, the contemporary period has been one of enormous growth in political opportunities available to women.

Women in State Legislatures

From the immediate post-suffrage period right up until the present time, state legislatures have been important political offices for women. Since the 1920s, more women have run for, and served in, state legislatures than Congress. Historically, the most significant time of change with regard to the number of women serving in state legislatures was from 1920 to 1925, the first five years after the passage of the federal suffrage amendment.[25] After that, the number of women running for and serving in state legislatures has undergone some fluctuations, fluctuations that in many ways mirror aspects of the social and political world around them. The Depression years saw a drop in the number of women seeking state legislative office, which was followed by a significant increase during World War II. After the war, periods of economic and social unrest served to decrease the candidate pool for state legislature (as least among women) until there was another jump in numbers after the Korean war. Emmy Werner makes the argument that the success of women candidates for state legislative office closely matched the way that the public perceived women and their appropriate role in society, suggesting that the public was more open to women candidates during times of social and economic calm but being more negative to their presence during times of national stress or crisis.[26] The more contemporary period of the past 40 years or so has witnessed a

TABLE 2.1:
Number of Women Candidates for National and State Offices
1970–2002

	U.S. Congress	Governor	State Legislator
1970	26	0	—
1972	34	0	—
1974	47	3	1125
1976	55	2	1258
1978	48	1	1348
1980	57	0	1426
1982	58	2	1643
1984	75	1	1756
1986	70	8	1813
1988	61	2	1853
1990	77	8	2064
1992	117	3	2375
1994	121	10	2285
1996	129	6	2274
1998	131	10	2280
2000	128	5	2228
2002	135	10	2345

Source: Center for the American Woman and Politics (CAWP), Eagleton Institute of Politics, Rutgers University, 2002.

tremendous change in the number of women running and serving in state legislatures. In 1975, 1,125 women ran for state legislative positions, and 610 were elected. By 2002, the number of women running had doubled to 2,228, and the number serving had almost tripled to 1,681.[27]

State legislatures have long been considered to be of particular importance to women by those who study women's progress in politics. They are
important for a number of reasons. First, state legislatures have been the
level of office in which women candidates have had the greatest amount of
success: More women have been elected to state legislative office than any
other elected office in the United States. In 2002, 1,680 women served as
state legislators, far more than the number of women who have served in
Congress since the first woman was elected in 1917.[28] But state legislatures
are considered important offices for women for more substantive reasons
as well. R. Darcy, Susan Welch, and Janet Clark suggest that state legislatures hold special importance to women because these bodies are primarily
responsible for handling many of the issues that are of central consequence
to women: equal rights, spousal abuse, rape, divorce and family law, abortion, and equal pay.[29] Finally, service in state legislatures can help place
women candidates in the pipeline for higher office. Few successful candidates, women or men, begin their political careers by running for U.S. Congress or the presidency. Instead, the path to success in American politics is
to build a career beginning with lower elected offices and moving up
through the ranks. State legislative service is a particularly important cre-
dential for a legitimate run for statewide office, such as for governor or for
Congress. More women serving in state legislatures means a larger pool of
potential candidates for other offices down the road.

Election to Congress—Widows and Sacrificial Lambs

After suffrage, women candidates began a slow entry into various elected
offices at the local and state legislative level. However, there was no corresponding increase in the number of women who served in Congress. Indeed, for much of the twentieth century, women's experiences in running
for and serving in Congress have been shaped by two forces: the widow
tradition and sacrificial lamb candidacies.

Jeannette Rankin, the first woman elected to Congress, only served until
1919, although she returned to the House of Representatives for a second
term in 1941. She was followed by 12 women who entered in the 1920s
and 11 women who entered in the 1930s. Most of these women stayed no
more than a term or two, and many of them gained their office through
what has become known as the "widow tradition."

The widow tradition refers to the habit political parties had of appointing a sympathetic family member, usually the widow, to serve out the term of a member who had died in office. This was viewed as an acceptable public role for a woman because she would be carrying on her late husband's work, not seeking political power in her own right. Appointing the widow was often done with the understanding that she would complete the term but not seek to be reelected in her own right. Instead, the parties would nominate another candidate, usually a man, who had no connection to the deceased member. For many of the early women in Congress, this was the most likely method of entrance into the House. Indeed, as Irwin Gertzog indicates, from 1916 to 1940, 54 percent of the women who served in the House succeeded their husbands, meaning that a minority of women members in this period entered on their own rights. Over time, fewer women have come into Congress in this way, although it was still a significant trend until the 1960s. From 1941 to 1964, 37 percent of women serving were widows. After 1964, this figure fell to about 15 percent. As of 2002, 45 of the 213 women who had served in Congress, fully 21 percent of all women members, had come to Congress through this path.

Although the widow tradition describes the method of entry for many women who have served in Congress, there was another phenomenon at work during the twentieth century that shaped the *possibility* of serving for many women candidates. This phenomenon has been referred to as the "sacrificial lamb" candidacy. As was discussed earlier, women candidates have often been nominated by parties in situations where that woman has very little chance of winning. The most common scenario might be one in which the minority party in a district or state nominates a woman candidate, thereby satisfying a desire to demonstrate diversity to the public while saving more winnable seats for male candidates.

Another circumstance involving a sacrificial lamb candidacy would be a person challenging a long-serving or popular incumbent. Certainly, the term sacrificial lamb does not only apply to women. Since men have historically made up the vast majority of candidates in American politics, there are plenty of men who have run for office as sacrificial lambs. But, in focusing on women's candidacies, historians and political observers have detected a pattern of parties being more willing to run women for office when the prospects of winning are low than when they are high. The work of Irwin Gertzog and M. Michele Simard on what they term "hopeless" candidacies for Congress illustrates this phenomenon. They define hopeless candidacies as those who run against incumbents or those who run as the nominee of a party that received less than 40 percent of the vote in earlier elections. In examining all women candidates from 1916 to 1978 and a sample of men candidates for the same period, they conclude that women were more likely than men to be nominated for hopeless races. This pattern holds true regardless of the time period considered or the party of the woman candidate.[30]

In the contemporary period, the picture for women standing for election to Congress has been a more positive one. Recent analysis of election returns indicates that women candidates for the House and the Senate are experiencing success rates equal to that of men candidates. Work by Jody Newman and her colleagues suggests that analysis of the situation facing women candidates for Congress has failed to account for the status of the candidates.[31] By this they mean whether a candidate is running as an incumbent, as a challenger to an incumbent, or as a candidate seeking an open seat. When comparing women and men candidates from 1972 to 1994 based on the type of candidacy, they find that women are just as successful as similarly situated men. For example, during the period of study, women open seat candidates for the House of Representatives won 48 percent of their races. The figure for the comparable pool of men was 51 percent. Similar success rates are demonstrated for women and men incumbents and challengers. This research presents a picture of women's integration into Congress as one that rests on increasing the number of women who run for these offices. However, whereas there is evidence to demonstrate that women and men of comparable status do equally well at the ballot box, this doesn't mean that women and men are treated in the same way by voters or evaluated in the same ways. Important here is the way people evaluate women candidates and whether those evaluations systematically help or hurt women when they run for office.

Public Attitudes on Women in Politics

Key to the chances of women candidates being successful in seeking office is a set of positive attitudes toward a political role for women among the public. One of the major roadblocks to women candidates in earlier times was the widespread belief that politics was not an appropriate activity for women. A public that believes that a woman's place is in the home is unlikely to vote for any women candidates with the courage to run. However, if voters feel that women have an equal role to play in political life, they can use these attitudes as a baseline against which they can evaluate individual women candidates and decide if they are worthy of support. Holding more egalitarian attitudes about women in politics doesn't guarantee that a voter will choose a woman candidate, but it is essential to that voter's willingness to consider voting for a woman. As we will see, the increased success of women candidates during the past 30 years or so has been mirrored by a gradual shifting in attitudes about women's place in political life.

One way to determine public attitudes toward women in politics is to examine attitudes about the proper role for women in society. Since 1972, the National Election Study has explored these attitudes. Their question asks whether women should have an equal role with men in running business, industry, and government or whether their place is in the home. The question is asked with a 7-point scale, with a score of 1 indicating strong belief that women should have an equal role and a score of 7 representing a strong belief that women's place is in the home. For easier interpretation, Figure 2.1 presents the data for the percentage of people who say that they support women having an equal role in society. Over the years, there has been consistent movement in the direction of people expressing support for an egalitarian position. In 1972, 47 percent of people believed women should have an equal role, 29 percent said women's place was in the home, and 19 percent put themselves in the middle of these two positions. In 2000, support for women's equal role in society had increased to 78 percent, with 11 percent taking the middle position, and 9 percent saying women's place is in the home. Again, change has occurred in favor of more egalitarian attitudes toward women in politics, but as many as one in five Americans may see the political world as an inappropriate place for women.

We have a good sense of the public's assessment of the place of women in political office going back to the 1930s, when the scientific study of public opinion was getting its start. Several organizations have measured these attitudes for a number of years, charting the evolution of people's ideas about what is right for women and for politics. Among the earliest of these were surveys conducted by the American Institute for Public Opinion, later the Gallup organization, on people's attitudes about the question of a woman president. In 1936, in response to a question that asked, "Would

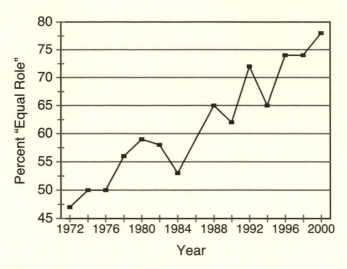

Figure 2.1: Attitudes Toward Women's Place in Society 1972–2000

you vote for a woman for president if she was qualified in every other respect?" 65 percent of the public said no.[32] Readers should note that the
wording of the question reveals much about the way women's political role
was perceived at this point in time. The phrase "if she was qualified in every
other respect" clearly implies that the major way in which she isn't qualified
is because she is a woman.

The wording of the question has changed over time, reflecting a move
away from an automatic assumption that a woman's sex was her disqualifying trait, to the present form that asks "If your party nominated a generally well-qualified person for president who happened to be a woman,
would you vote for that person?" Figure 2.2 traces responses to the question about a woman president through the present day. The data clearly
show that the American people have gradually changed their thinking
about whether they would vote for a woman candidate for our nation's
highest office, starting with a minority of people being willing to do so in
1937 to the vast majority in the contemporary period indicating that they
would. However, in 2000, when asked, all else being equal, whether a
woman or a man would make a better president, 42 percent of survey respondents chose a man, 31 percent a woman, and 22 percent said candidate sex would not matter to performance in office.[33]

Of course, it should be noted that a woman major-party candidate for president in the United States has been a hypothetical situation during the entire period in which this question has been asked. It may be that survey respondents are more comfortable expressing what they perceive is the socially acceptable answer rather than revealing any concerns about a woman president. For this reason, it seems reasonable to suspect that these questions about a woman president probably overestimate support for women candidates.

Although certainly an interesting benchmark for people's attitudes about women in politics, the question of a woman president may still be too artificial to reflect accurately the public's level of comfort with women in elected office. Perhaps a better measure of the willingness of people to support women candidates for office focuses on their election in general. Since 1975, the Gallup organization has asked people whether they thought the country would be governed better or governed worse if more women held political office. Table 2.2 indicates that in 1975, 33 percent of respondents said we would be governed better, 18 percent said things would be worse, and 38 percent said it would make no difference. The reasons that people gave for thinking that women would be a positive or a negative influence in government are illustrative. People who thought more women officeholders would lead to better government said this because they saw women as more reliable and conscientious, less corrupt, and less easily manipulated than men. They also said that women would be more likely to think about social justice, peaceful solutions to international problems, poor people, and fiscal responsibility.

Those who thought more women in government would make things worse said so because they believed that women's place was in the home; that government was a man's job; and that women would be too soft, too flighty and inconsistent, and not business-minded enough. Each of these sets of very different evaluations of women and their abilities conforms to stereotypes, both positive and negative, about women's natures.[34] As we will see in Chapter 3, the public still holds these sorts of stereotyped attitudes about the abilities of women in office.

In 1984, 28 percent of respondents saw more women in office as positive, and 15 percent thought it would be negative. Both of these figures are lower than the corresponding ones for 1975. Indeed, the difference between the

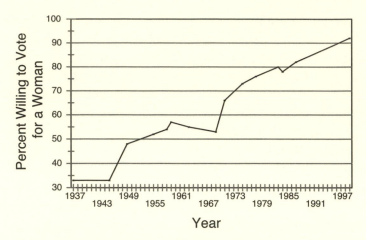

Figure 2.2: Public Willingness to Vote for a Woman Candidate for President 1937–1999

two years is the increase in the percentage of people who said more women would make no difference, 38 percent in 1975 and 46 percent in 1984. But by 2000, a remarkable shift had taken place when fully 57 percent of people surveyed said more women in government would be a positive for our country. Seventeen percent said this would make things worse, and only 20 percent saw no difference between women and men.[35] At a time when women's participation in elected office is at an all-time high, it is clear that the public sees this trend as positive, perhaps signaling a situation on which women candidates can capitalize. Interestingly, in line with what researchers refer to as the "affinity effect," women are somewhat more likely than men to say that more women in office would make a positive difference in each time period, and this gap was wider in 2000 than in 1975 or 1984.

Changes Among Women Bring
Changes for Women Candidates

The evolution of attitudes toward women candidates is an interesting one in that it parallels the evolution of women's roles in American society. Tom Smith, in analyzing Gallup public opinion poll data on support for a woman president from 1936 to 1974, finds a pattern of change in that support that mirrors larger societal debates about women's place.[36] (See Figure

TABLE 2.2:
Public Attitudes Toward Having More Women in Elected Office
1975–2000

		Better	Worse	No Difference
All Adults	1975	33%	18%	38%
	1984	28%	15%	46%
	2000	57%	17%	20%
Women	1975	36%	20%	34%
	1984	32%	14%	44%
	2000	64%	14%	14%
Men	1975	29%	17%	43%
	1984	24%	15%	48%
	2000	50%	20%	25%

The question posed was, "Do you think this country would be governed better or governed worse if more women were in political office?"

Source: Gallup Poll, January 4, 2001.

2.2.) For example, he notes a gradual increase in support for a woman president from 1936 to 1945, but then a steep increase from 1945 to 1949. During the prewar period, he suggests, the role of wife and mother was still firmly held as the most appropriate for women. But, during World War II, women's activities in the labor market, the military, and the community dramatically altered public attitudes toward women's role in society, which may help explain the steep increase in reported support for a woman president. After the immediate postwar period, beginning in 1949, there is a focus on the revitalization of the family; many women returned home, and the birthrate soared. Correspondingly, support for a woman for president slowed, beginning a gradual rise until about 1969. Then, in the period from 1969 to 1974, there is another sharp increase in support, which comports with the beginnings of the modern women's movement, women's increased labor force and educational participation, and a decline in fertility.

As women continued to expand their roles in the public sphere during the 1970s and 1980s, support for a woman president steadily increased. Then, between 1987 and 1999, support for a woman president jumped 10 percentage points to its current level of 92 percent. During this same time period, women's integration into educational and occupational arenas increased alongside this support. Table 2.3 presents data on the increased participation in areas that provide important credentials for people who want to pursue elected office. Women in the United States now earn more than half of the bachelor's degrees awarded and have dramatically increased their share of postgraduate degrees of all types since the 1970s.[37] Particularly important here are law degrees because law is one of the primary backgrounds for candidates for state legislatures and Congress. The figures for women's participation in the labor force tell the same story: Since the 1970s, women have been increasingly likely to be employed outside the home in full-time positions, another important avenue for obtaining the requisite credentials to be a legitimate political candidate.[38]

It is no accident, then, that the number of women candidates for such offices as Congress and state legislatures begins a steady and significant increase in the 1970s, continuing through the present time period. In the last 30 years or so, women have been increasingly involved in the professional activities that help them mount serious candidacies for office. This has led to an increase in the number of women serving in these offices. As the public observes more women in public life and in political office, they may well become more comfortable with politics as an appropriate venue for women, which can translate into expressed support for an eventual woman president.

Structural Barriers

The primary focus of this project is on the relationship between the public and women candidates. However, this relationship is not the only important one in terms of explaining how women candidates have fared over time. Indeed, an explanation for the current underrepresentation of women in elected office in the United States has several elements, some that are important in a historical sense and others that are still influential today.

TABLE 2.3:
Trends in Women's Educational and Occupational Advancement

<u>Education</u>

Percentage of Postsecondary Degrees Earned by Women by Level of Degree

	<u>1976</u>	<u>1996</u>
Bachelor's	46%	55%
Master's	46%	56%
Law	23%	44%
Medicine	19%	41%
Doctoral	23%	40%

<u>Occupation</u>

Women in the Labor Force

	<u>1976</u>	<u>1996</u>
Women's Participation	47%	60%
Women as Percentage of Total	41%	46%
Year Round/Full Time Work	40%	56%

Women Lawyers as Percentage of All Lawyers

<u>1976</u>	<u>1996</u>
5%	25%

Source: *The American Woman 2001–2002.* Cynthia Costello and Anne Stone. New York: W. W. Norton, 2001.

One of the earliest treatments of women's underrepresentation in political life was written in 1955 by Maurice Duverger.[39] He suggested that there were three major barriers women faced when running for office. The first, voter hostility, has been addressed in this chapter and will be considered throughout the rest of the book. Clearly, it is safe to say that hostility toward women candidates has stemmed from the widespread belief that public life was inappropriate for women. Also as clearly, this way of thinking about women has changed considerably over time. The data on support for a hypothetical woman candidate for president and the attitudes on women's roles in society demonstrate that the public is more likely to embrace egalitarian attitudes toward women today than at any point in our nation's history. Yet this is not to suggest that there is no bias among the public, only that levels of bias are low enough to no longer provide a significant impediment to women's chances of election.

A more contemporary consideration that can influence how the public views women candidates is their treatment by the media. In most elections, people obtain their information about political candidates not through direct contact with those candidates but as a result of hearing or reading something about them in the media. As a result, the way the media presents information about women candidates can have a significant impact on the impressions that people form about them. There is extensive evidence compiled during the past 15 years or so that demonstrates that the media often treats women candidates differently than it does men. This differential treatment tends to occur both in the amount and the content of media coverage of women. First, women candidates often receive less coverage than their male opponents, which can limit the ability of voters to learn about these women.[40]

Second, with regard to content, coverage of women is often more likely to focus on their viability (or lack thereof) than is coverage of men. Kim Kahn suggests that this focus on whether women can win can leave an impression in people's minds that they can't, that women candidates are somehow less viable than are men candidates.[41] The other way in which the content of media treatment of women candidates is different from that of men is in the greater likelihood that coverage of women will center on personal issues, such as appearance, personality, marriage, and family status, or on gender-stereotyped issues. Media coverage that provides information on irrelevant details or on a narrow set of policy issues can reinforce stereotyped impressions that voters may have about women candidates and may make these candidates appear less serious than their male opponents.[42]

The second major barrier to women's success identified by Duverger was the political party system. Parties are crucial gatekeepers in the electoral process through their power to recruit and support candidates for election. Duverger reasoned that the male-dominated party structure would not be welcoming of new groups and would work to limit their participation. He dubbed this the "male conspiracy." More contemporary research describes an "outgroup effect" in which party leaders may evaluate individual women candidates by using more general assumptions about women as a group. David Niven's study of county-level party leaders and potential women candidates uncovered continuing resistance to the recruitment of women candidates in some places, with a majority of the women he interviewed describing some experience of discrimination at the hands of party leaders.[43]

Other authors, who might ascribe less overt bias against women to party leaders, suggest that party elites are more likely to recruit candidates from among people similar to themselves.[44] Under either condition, this line of reasoning suggests that women are less likely than men to receive significant recruitment attention from political parties. However, in recent elections, as women candidates have received more attention from the media and the public, parties have made more affirmative efforts to broaden their appeal and to present a more diverse set of candidates for office. Indeed, at the last two presidential nominating conventions, both the Democrats and Republicans made significant efforts to show off their women candidates for Congress and other offices.

The third aspect of Duverger's analysis was the barriers to women's advancement that resulted from electoral arrangements. Here he argued that various aspects of electoral systems can make it easier or more difficult for women to be elected. In the United States there are several relevant considerations. First, there is research that suggests that the U.S. election system makes a difference for the election of women. For example, at the state legislative level, women candidates are more likely to be elected in places that use a multimember district format than in those that employ a single-member district system.[45] There are a few states in the United States that use a mixed multimember and single-member district format, but most state legislators are elected from single-member districts. Also, Congress is organized through single-member districts. So some piece of women's underrepresentation may be explained by the election rules adopted in the United States.

Another aspect of the electoral system, though not one that was as significant in Duverger's time, is the important role of money in campaigns and elections. Running for office in the United States is an expensive enterprise, and a candidate's potential for success, in part, rests on how much money she can raise. Historically, women have had some trouble tapping into fund-raising networks and raising the money necessary to make them viable candidates. But, as the number of women candidates has increased in the 1980s and 1990s, the amount of money women can raise has increased as well. In arguing that women are no longer disadvantaged in terms of fund-raising, Barbara Burrell demonstrates that many women candidates for the House of Representatives have been raising and spending *more* money than their male opponents in recent years.[46]

Perhaps the most significant system barrier to increasing the number of women officeholders is the influence of incumbency. At every level of American politics, incumbents are overwhelmingly likely to win reelection. Indeed, in seeking reelection to Congress, approximately 96 percent of House members and 85 percent of senators will be successful. This is because of the tremendous advantages that incumbency brings: campaign money, media attention, and name recognition. The incumbency advantage is no stronger for men than for women: Women incumbents are returned to office at the same rate as men incumbents.[47] But the reality for women candidates is that the vast majority of incumbents at every level of office are men. Fifty-seven women incumbent House members ran and were reelected in 2002, but that number is small compared to the 357 men incumbents who did the same. This means that opportunities for breaking into office by running for open seats are limited, both for women and men.

When Duverger looked at the situation facing women candidates in the 1950s, he saw significant impediments to their success. Many of these aspects have changed over time, either becoming less considerable barriers or, in some circumstances, becoming advantages to women. However, the reality of the success of women candidates is not governed simply by one or the other of these influences. Instead, as we will see, the way that candidate sex and gender issues play out in elections is rather complex.

Conclusion

This chapter began with quotes from two well-known political men, John Bailey and Moon Landrieu, on the limited role available to women in political life and public office. Perhaps the best way to end the chapter, and to illustrate the evolution of women's role in politics, is to discuss two well-known political women: Barbara Kennelly and Mary Landrieu. Barbara Kennelly began her career in elected office in 1975 by serving on the Hartford (CT) common council. She was then elected secretary of state of Connecticut, before being elected to the U.S. House of Representatives. She served in the House for 16 years, retiring in 1998 to run for governor of Connecticut, a race she lost. In 1979, at the age of 23, Mary Landrieu was elected to the Louisiana House of Representatives. After serving two terms, she was elected state treasurer. In 1996, she was elected as the first woman to represent Louisiana in the U.S. Senate. Barbara Kennelly is the daughter of John Bailey. Moon Landrieu, as you may have guessed by now, was Mary Landrieu's father.

Notes

1. Dinkin, Robert, *Before Equal Suffrage: Women in Partisan Politics from Colonial Times to 1920* (Westport, Conn.: Greenwood Press, 1995), p. 8

2. Ibid., p. 16.

3. Ibid., p. 41.

4. Ibid., p. 43.

5. Ibid.

6. Edwards, Rebecca, *Angels in the Machinery: Gender in American Party Politics from the Civil War to the Progressive Era* (New York: Oxford Press, 1997).

7. Ibid.

8. Matthews, Glenna, *The Rise of Public Woman: Women's Power and Women's Place in the United States, 1930–1970* (New York: Oxford University Press, 1992); Silleto, John, and Constance Lieber, "Martha Maria Hughes Cannon," in *Utah History Encyclopedia*, ed. Allan Kent Powell (Salt Lake City: University of Utah Press, 1994).

9. Dinkin 1995, p. 107.

10. Freeman, Jo, *A Room at a Time: How Women Entered Party Politics* (Lanham, Md.: Rowman and Littlefield Press, 2000).

11. Kaptur, Marcy, *Women of Congress: A Twentieth-Century Odyssey* (Washington, D.C.: Congressional Quarterly, 1996), p. 25.

12. Foerstel, Karen, *Biographical Directory of Congressional Women* (Westport, Conn.: Greenwood Press, 1999).

13. Anthony, Susan B., and Ida Harper, *History of Woman Suffrage*, Vol. 4 (New York: Arno Press, 1969).

14. Andersen, Kristi, *After Suffrage: Women in Partisan and Electoral Politics Before the New Deal* (Chicago: University of Chicago Press, 1996), p. 122.

15. Ibid.

16. Ibid., p. 119.

17. Ibid., p. 116.

18. Andersen 1996, p. 130

19. Ibid., p. 133.

20. Deutsch, Sarah Jane. "From Ballots to Breadlines: 1920–1940," in *No Small Courage: A History of Women in the United States*, ed. Nancy Cott (New York: Oxford University Press, 2000).

21. Andersen 1996, p. 124.

22. As evidence of the "male" nature of politics during this time period, consider the text of a survey question asked by the Gallup organization in 1955: "If you had a son, would you like to see him go into politics as a life's work?" The Gallup Poll, February 10–15, 1955.

23. Hartmann, Susan, *The Home Front and Beyond: American Women in the 1940s* (Boston: Twayne Publishers, 1982), p. 152.

24. Center for the American Woman and Politics (CAWP), *Fact Sheet*, "Women in State Legislatures 2002, Women in the U.S. Congress 2002" (New Brunswick, N.J.: Eagleton Institute of Politics, Rutgers University, 2002); Center for the American Woman and Politics (CAWP), *Fact Sheet*, "Summary of Women Candidates for Selected Offices 1970–2000" (New Brunswick, N.J.: Eagleton Institute of Politics, Rutgers University, 2002).

25. Werner, Emmy, "Women in the State Legislatures," *Western Political Quarterly* 21 (1968):40–50.

26. Ibid.

27. Center for the American Woman and Politics (CAWP), *Fact Sheet*, "Summary of Women Candidates For Selected Offices: 1970–2000" (New Brunswick, N.J.: Eagleton Institute of Politics, Rutgers University, 2000).

28. This is, in part, because there are more state legislative positions than any other.

29. Darcy, R., Susan Welch, and Janet Clark, *Women, Elections, and Representation*. 2nd ed. (Lincoln, Nebr.: University of Nebraska Press, 1994).

30. Gertzog, Irwin, and M. Michele Simard, "Women and 'Hopeless' Congressional Candidates: Nominations Frequency, 1916–1978," *American Politics Quarterly* 9:449–466.

31. Seltzer, Richard, Jody Newman, and Melissa Leighton, *Sex as a Political Variable: Women as Candidates and Voters in U.S. Elections* (Boulder: Lynne Rienner, 1997).

32. Smith, Tom, "A Study of Trends in the Political Role of Women, 1936–1974," in *Studies of Social Change Since 1948*, ed. James A. Davis, NONC Report 127B (Chicago: NONC, 1979), pp. 215–254.

33. Simmons, Wendy, "A Majority of Americans Say More Women in Political Office Would Be Positive for the Country," *The Gallup Poll Monthly*, January 2001.

34. Ibid.

35. Ibid., p. 8.

36. Smith, Tom, 1979, p. 240.

37. Costello, Cynthia, and Anne Stone, *The American Woman 2001–2002* (New York: W. W. Norton, 2001).

38. Ibid.

39. Duverger, Maurice, *The Political Role of Women* (Paris: UNESCO, 1955).

40. Kahn, Kim, *The Political Consequences of Being a Woman* (New York: Columbia University Press, 1996).

41. Ibid.

42. Devitt, James, *Framing Gender on the Campaign Trail: Women's Executive Leadership and the Press* (Philadelphia: Annenberg Public Policy Center, University of Pennsylvania, 2000); Jamieson, Kathleen Hall, *The Double Bind: Women and Leadership* (New York, Oxford University Press, 1995).

43. Niven, David, "Party Elites and Women Candidates: The Shape of Bias," *Women and Politics* 19 (1998):57–80.

44. Prewitt, Kenneth, *The Recruitment of Political Leaders* (Indianapolis: Bobbs-Merrill, 1970).

45. Darcy, Welch, and Clark 1994.

46. Burrell, Barbara, *A Woman's Place Is in the House: Campaigning for Congress in the Feminist Era* (Ann Arbor: University of Michigan Press, 1994).

47. Seltzer, Newman, and Leighton 1997.

3

Evaluations of Women Candidates

THE FIRST WAY TO EXAMINE HOW voters respond to women candidates is to get a better sense for how they evaluate them. Certainly, voting for (or against) a woman candidate can be a sign of support (or rejection), but that is really an imprecise measure of a voter's evaluation. As we will see in Chapters 4 and 5, a person's vote choice can be influenced by several factors, and determining which factors are most important is not always easy. So, even though vote choice regarding women candidates is one way to determine people's levels of acceptance of these women, it is not a complete one. We begin by investigating how people think about women, how they evaluate them when asked to, and how they assess their abilities.

Stereotypes

Stereotyping is a common psychological process by which individuals evaluate the world around them. According to social psychological theory, people, through direct experience or other exposure, develop beliefs about the characteristics (usually personality traits and behaviors) of social groups. This knowledge influences their evaluations of individuals who are members of these groups.[1] Once an individual assigns an object to a particular social group, he or she then attributes the relevant characteristics of that group to the object.[2] This process, known as categorization, is useful to individuals for several reasons. First, people exist in a complex, information-rich world that can sometimes be overwhelming. Stereotypes are useful for evaluating a person or an object based on limited information because their use does not require a great deal of specific information about each particular object being judged. For example, if a voter learns that a particular candidate is a Republican, she might conclude that the candidate's position on abortion is pro-life and that the candidate is opposed to a government-run health care system. It is more efficient (and probably easier) to categorize people or objects by their similarities and differences and draw conclusions based on these decisions.

The opposite of stereotyping, relying on specific information about an object to draw conclusions, is more difficult, given the typical constraints on the amount and quality of information available to the average person. It may be the case that this particular Republican candidate is pro-choice, but determining that would usually require more time and effort than simply making an assumption based on party identification. This tendency to rely on stereotypes may be particularly applicable when we consider politics, which is often outside the realm of daily activity for most people. When evaluating political parties, policies, or individual candidates, people often have relatively little information on which to base an impression. Therefore, people develop a judgment or evaluation based on whatever information *is* readily available, whether it is party affiliation, ideology, race, sex, or any of a number of other categorizing frameworks individuals could employ.

Sex Stereotypes

Because stereotyping occurs when people generalize about an individual based on easily learned characteristics, it makes sense that sex stereotypes are among the most pervasive. Given the general definition of stereotypes discussed above, sex stereotypes are those beliefs about the personal traits of women and men that are linked to the categories "female" and "male." (Recall from Chapter 1 the distinction between biological sex and the culturally defined categories of feminine and masculine.) Work on sex stereotypes has demonstrated that typical female qualities include warmth, expressiveness, gentleness, compassion, and emotion. Men are perceived as strong, competent, rational, aggressive, and knowledgeable.[3] A recent study suggests that sex stereotypes are a cross-cultural phenomenon, with evidence of their content and application coming from a ten-nation study that included Australia, Brazil, Norway, Pakistan, Peru, and the United States.[4]

Other work on sex stereotypes makes the link between beliefs about women and men and the roles each sex plays in society. Because women and men take on somewhat different roles in society, the traits ascribed to each are, in some ways, a function of the roles they play. Women are over-represented in support, caretaking, and nurturing roles, which then contributes to all women being seen as nurturing, compassionate, and caring. Men, who are more likely to be employed in jobs that require action, rationality, and leadership, become identified with the characteristics of the positions they hold. As further evidence of the link between sex and social role, this work demonstrates that men holding traditionally female positions were stereotyped with the female traits—caring, warm, expressive—which suggests that role stereotypes can outweigh sex stereotypes.[5] Finally, sex stereotypes can often become a self-fulfilling prophecy. Studies indicate that people can change their behavior to conform to the stereotyped expectations of others. For example, one study demonstrated that women behaved in a more sex-stereotyped manner when they interacted with men they were told held traditional views of women than when they were paired with men who supposedly held less traditional views. A similar study examined the behavior of job applicants who were told that their interviewers held more sexist views.[6] As we will see, many aspects of the operation of general sex stereotypes are relevant to a more detailed examination of how the public evaluates women and men in the political world.

Political Stereotypes of Women and Men

Since the 1970s, the General Social Survey (GSS) has asked respondents a series of questions that try to determine how the public thinks about the emotional characteristics and social roles of women and men as they relate to politics. The question dealing with emotional characteristics asks respondents to "Tell me if you agree or disagree with this statement: Most men are better suited emotionally for politics than are most women." As Table 3.1 demonstrates, agreement with this perspective has run from 47 percent of survey respondents in 1974 to about 23 percent in 1998. With regard to social roles, the GSS asks "Do you agree or disagree with this statement: Women should take care of running their homes and leave running the country up to men." In 1974, 36 percent of the public agreed that politics was not appropriate for women. By 1998, this number had dropped to 15 percent. Although each of these questions demonstrates an evolution in the public's thinking about women, today anywhere from one-fifth to one-quarter of the public willingly expresses concern about the abilities of women in the political arena.

TABLE 3.1:
Emotional and Social Stereotypes About Women, Men, and Politics
General Social Survey 1974–1998

	1974	1978	1983	1988	1993	1998
Agree	47%	43%	36%	32%	22%	23%
Disagree	53%	57%	64%	68%	78%	77%

Question 202A: Tell me if you agree or disagree with this statement: Most men are better suited emotionally for politics than most women.

	1974	1978	1983	1988	1993	1998
Agree	36%	31%	23%	21%	15%	15%
Disagree	64%	69%	77%	79%	85%	85%

Question 199: Do you agree or disagree with this statement: Women should take care of running their homes and leave running the country up to men.

Source: General Social Survey.

These questions tap into people's ideas about men's and women's behavior: how each might act in a public setting; how they would handle the compromise, confrontation, and persuasion that is at the heart of politics; perhaps even how women and men would behave in a crisis. It is not terribly difficult to imagine people who agreed with the statement conjuring up images of the rational, steady, even-keeled man and comparing him to the more emotional, unpredictable woman. In doing so, they would be relying on stereotypes about what women and men are like. Even people who disagreed with the premise of the question probably started with the same vision of women's and men's emotional traits before rejecting them as inaccurate. In either case, the question stimulates those who hear it to think about people as members of groups (women, men) and then think about what they believe about members of those groups (emotional, rational). This is one small illustration of how people think about women and men in the political world, by relying on stereotypes.

In developing an extensive literature on women candidates for elective office, political scientists have demonstrated that the public looks at women and men in politics in predictably stereotypic ways. These stereotyped assessments of political leaders and candidates focus on three major areas: ideology, personality characteristics, and issue specialization.

One of the more enduring stereotypes of women politicians and candidates is that they are more liberal than men. Several recent research studies have confirmed this finding. As has been discussed previously, much of the research on evaluations of women candidates has been carried out using experiments and hypothetical election scenarios or extremely small, geographically limited samples of voters. For example, Deborah Alexander and Kristi Andersen found that voters in upstate New York perceived hypothetical women candidates as much more liberal than hypothetical male candidates, whereas Leonie Huddy and Nayda Terkildsen found the same beliefs about women candidates' ideology among undergraduate students involved in an election experiment.[7] Other work has employed surveys to ask more representative groups of people about their impressions of hypothetical women candidates, each finding that voters see women candidates, regardless of party, as more liberal than men.[8] This last finding, that even Republican women candidates are seen as more liberal than Republican men, points to the way that sex stereotypes can interact with, and perhaps moderate, partisan stereotypes. Finally, recent research by Koch has moved our understanding of the public's impressions of women candidates forward by demonstrating that, not only are women candidates of both parties seen as more liberal than their male counterparts, but they are perceived as more liberal than they actually are.[9] Koch makes the argument that these inaccurate assessments of women candidates' ideology can have consequences at the polls. Given that most voters consider themselves to be ideologically moderate, the perceived liberalism of Democratic women candidates moves them further away from the average voter, reducing the chances that they would receive votes. However, the exaggerated liberalism of Republican women candidates actually moves them closer to the average voter, who may then be more likely to choose that woman candidate.

One interesting aspect of voters' tendencies to see women candidates as more liberal than men is the fairly significant evidence that they *are* often more liberal than men.[10] Voters may be stereotyping women candidates based on some more general sex stereotypes about women's nature, but in this instance, there is some correspondence between the stereotype and reality. Alternatively, the public may not be employing a stereotype of women so much as they are reacting to the information they take in about these women through the media, campaign events, and the like, although given the relatively limited information most people have about politics and political candidates, this is the less likely explanation.

Another way in which voters stereotype women candidates is by ascribing to them certain character traits. Here again the literature is clear. The public sees women candidates as warm, compassionate, kind, and passive, whereas men are perceived as strong, knowledgeable, tough, direct, and assertive.[11] Again, these ideas reflect the more general stereotypes about women that people tend to hold.[12] The importance of stereotypes is demonstrated by research that suggests that women candidates are evaluated as warm and tender even when the messages they are sending to the public are more tough and "masculine."[13] Concern about these trait stereotypes of women candidates is raised because of the assumed gulf between character traits seen as "feminine" and the skills and abilities generally considered to be important in public office. If women aren't viewed as demonstrating important leadership abilities, perhaps voters will not consider them for office. Indeed, several experimental studies indicate that people often value traits considered to be masculine more highly when considering what a "good politician" should be like. They also consider these masculine qualities to be more important as the level of office they are considering rises from local to national.[14] However, because these findings all come from experimental settings with hypothetical candidates, we need to exercise caution in assuming that things work the same way in actual elections.

The final major type of stereotype that voters connect with women candidates is a set of beliefs about their policy interest and expertise. Flowing from the ideology and personality stereotypes people hold, they most commonly associate women candidates and officeholders with what are often called the "compassion" issues—poverty, health care, the elderly, education, children and family issues, and the environment. Men, not surprisingly, are seen as more concerned with economics, defense, business, crime, and agriculture.[15] As with trait stereotypes, some people express concern that voters may actively use these judgments about women's and men's perceived policy differences against women candidates. For example, if women are not perceived to be as competent to handle crime or economic issues, voters who are primarily concerned about these issues may reject women candidates as inappropriate for office.

This concern, although potentially valid, raises the question of whether the opposite might also be true. If stereotypes about ideology or traits or issue competency can work against women candidates, are there not also times when they might work in their favor? Are stereotypes always harmful to women candidates? There is evidence to suggest that the answer is no. Some voters may not choose a woman candidate because she is thought to lack the toughness or experience to deal with military issues. But other voters, who value education or social issues more highly, may actually be drawn to women candidates because of their stereotyped strengths. And although men are usually stereotyped as being tougher and more decisive than women, women candidates are perceived as being more honest and more competent than men and are often seen as "outsiders" to politics.[16] This can be a valuable asset for women candidates in times when voter dissatisfaction with government and incumbent leaders is high. For example, in 1992, women candidates for Congress attracted votes from those who were most dissatisfied with sitting incumbents.[17]

Women candidates are also perceived to be much better at addressing issues of special concern to women than are men. On such issues as sexual harassment, abortion, and women's rights, women are judged to be more competent.[18] When women's issues are particularly salient for the public (or at least one half of the public), voters may seek out women candidates to ensure action on these issues. There is ample evidence that the 1991 Senate confirmation hearing for Supreme Court Justice Clarence Thomas, which highlighted the issue of workplace sexual harassment, combined with the record number of women candidates for Congress in 1992, increased the attention to candidate sex that year. This focus on candidate sex and gender issues brightened the election prospects of women candidates, particularly among women voters.[19]

So even though some political observers raise concerns that public stereotypes can work against women at the polls, it is important to keep in mind that these stereotypes can also work in women's favor. How voters perceive women and men candidates is an important consideration in politics. But perhaps just as important is what voters perceive to be the important issues in any particular election and the qualities needed in leaders to address those issues. There are times, as recent history has shown, that stereotypes about women candidates can be in line with what the public is looking for from candidates, potentially giving women candidates an advantage.

Sex Stereotypes and Political Party

Much of what we know about the stereotypical impressions the public holds of women candidates comes from experimental research. The advantage of using an experimental framework for studying these questions is that researchers are able to isolate the specific impact of candidate sex on the evaluations subjects make. Many of these works present people with identical campaign information (speeches, newspaper articles, campaign commercials) for women and men candidates. If the only aspect of the experiment that varies is the sex of the candidate, researchers are able to isolate the impact of this variable on people's evaluations of women and men. All else held equal, people respond to women candidates in a particular way. But this same strength is a limitation in that all things are never equal in actual elections, and elections do not occur in a vacuum. Candidate sex is merely one of (potentially) many pieces of information voters may have about a candidate, and this piece of information is considered by voters alongside any other pieces of information they may possess.

One of the most significant considerations here is the question of how candidate sex interacts with political party. In the vast majority of elections in the United States, information about a candidate's party affiliation is readily available, if no other place than on the ballot itself. People hold partisan stereotypes in the same way that they hold sex stereotypes.[20] Because we know that party identification is a powerful influence on evaluations of candidates and vote choice, we then must address how and when candidate sex is relevant once we have considered political party. It may be that candidate sex, although an important influence on political decisions in isolation, loses some of its impact when it is measured against other important political variables.

This potential interaction is further complicated by the fact that most women candidates for Congress in the past 20 years have run as Democrats. From 1990 to 2000, the period of time under examination here, 60 percent of the women candidates for the Senate and 64 percent of the candidates for the House of Representatives ran as Democrats.[21] Given that people's stereotypes of the Democratic and Republican parties correspond in many ways to thinking about women and men (Democrats are better able to address social issues and poverty, whereas Republicans are more well-suited for economic and military policies), it may be the case that sex and party stereotypes can work to reinforce each other (as in the case of a woman Democrat) or offset each other (as with a woman Republican). A recent experimental study designed to focus on this potential interaction concludes that, in most instances, partisan cues overwhelmed all other sources of information about candidate beliefs and positions. In only one case, on handling of women's issues, did candidate sex exhibit any impact on people's evaluations of candidates.[22] So learning more about the evaluations people make of women who have run in actual elections, and what considerations they employ in making them, is an important step in understanding how candidate sex affects elections.

Evaluations of Women Candidates for Congress, 1990–2000

The National Election Study offers us three ways by which we can examine how the public evaluates women candidates in actual elections through a series of questions that ask respondents to provide evaluations of candidates for the House. Because the biennial NES surveys only ask these questions about candidates for the House of Representatives, the analysis presented in this chapter will focus exclusively on those races.

Political Ideology

As stated earlier in the chapter, there is fairly clear evidence that people often see women candidates as possessing a liberal political ideology. This stems from the stereotyped assumption that women are more nurturing and compassionate than are men. The National Election Study includes a question that allows us to examine whether respondents evaluating actual House candidates make such distinctions among women and men.

The first set of evaluations of House candidates that NES respondents make involves placing the Democratic and Republican candidates on a 7-point scale measuring political ideology. The scale is designed such that a score of 1 means that the candidate is perceived to be extremely liberal and 7 means that the candidate is seen as extremely conservative.[23] Experimental research on stereotypes would have us expect that women candidates would be evaluated as more liberal than men candidates. Because the questions in the survey ask respondents to evaluate the ideology of Democratic and Republican candidates separately, we will be comparing women and men within each of the parties. This necessity provides the added benefit of controlling for party stereotypes.

The model for this analysis includes several variables that are considered to be important determinants of the public's estimates of candidate ideological position. Of greatest interest to this discussion are the variables measuring whether the candidate being evaluated was a woman, an incumbent, or an incumbent woman. Factors other than stereotypical perceptions that may shape a person's evaluation of a candidate's ideology include respondents' ideology, their level of affect for the House candidate (as measured by the feeling thermometer score), an interaction between the feeling thermometer and respondent ideology, and respondents' perception of the sponsoring party's ideology.[24] Given past research suggesting that people are likely to project their own ideology onto candidates (especially those candidates they like) or are likely to employ category-based information when assessing individuals, we would expect that people's own ideology and their perceptions of party ideology will be related to their evaluation of candidates.

The analysis for political ideology is conducted in two ways, as all the analysis in this chapter will be. First, the data for all six House elections from 1990 to 2000 will be combined to allow for an examination of the trends in evaluations of women candidates in the contemporary period.[25] Then, the analysis will be carried out for each individual election year. This is necessary because each election is a unique event, shaped by the candidates, issues, and voters in that particular setting. To acknowledge the individual nature of elections, we need to consider whether trends that may appear in the pooled analysis are consistent over time or whether they are more episodic and tied to the conditions of a particular election.

The analysis outlined in this chapter, and throughout the book, employs a statistical technique called multiple regression analysis (or a variation on regression analysis). The aim of regression analysis is to understand the relationship between variables and to predict the value of one variable based on our knowledge of the values of others. We refer to the variable we are trying to explain or predict as the dependent variable and those things that form the explanation as the independent variables. For example, in this chapter we will examine the relationship between people's evaluations of congressional candidates (the dependent variable to be explained) and candidate sex (the independent variable that influences evaluations). However, in doing so we must acknowledge that people's evaluations of candidates are probably driven by more than just whether the candidate is a woman or a man. Therefore, we must consider the impact of other influences, such as a person's political party, education, or ideology on those evaluations. Using multiple regression analysis allows us to assess the contributions of one or more of these considerations on people's evaluations at the same time.

The tables in this book present regression coefficients for the variables in each analysis. These coefficients summarize how much a change in an independent variable will influence the dependent variable while holding the influence of all other independent variables constant. There are two main things of which to take note regarding these coefficients. The first is the direction of the coefficient, which is either positive or negative. A positive relationship is one in which change in an independent variable leads to change in the same direction in the dependent variable, whereas a negative relationship is one in which change in one direction in an independent variable leads to change in the opposite direction in the dependent variable. To use a general example, we might hypothesize that people with more education would be more likely to vote for a woman candidate. If true, this would be a positive relationship. However, if we find that people with less education are more likely to vote for a women, then we would have observed a negative relationship.

The second thing to notice in the analysis presented in the tables is whether a coefficient is significant or not, as noted by the asterisks located next to the coefficients. This tells us whether the relationship between the independent and dependent variables is a real one, that is, whether it is one in which we can have confidence. Because we cannot examine the relationship between the entire public's evaluations of every woman candidate, we must rely on studying a sample of people and candidates. Statistical significance assures us that a relationship that we observe in this sample will mirror the relationship in the "real world." Alternatively, a variable that is not significantly related to the dependent variable has no real impact on that variable.

To take an example from Table 3.2, note that the coefficient for the variable "woman candidate" in the column headed "Democrats" is -.377 and is statistically significant. In the data employed here, the variable measuring women candidates is coded 0 for no and 1 for yes. Ideology is measured on a seven-point scale coded 1 for extremely liberal and 7 for extremely conservative. The relationship between these variables is negative, which means that women candidates are evaluated as more liberal than are men. That this is a significant relationship means that in the population (beyond this sample), women candidates are seen as more liberal than men as well.

A final type of information the analysis provides is offered by the impact coefficient, which appears in parentheses in each table. This coefficient represents the change in a dependent variable as you move from the lowest to highest value of each independent variable. Taking our example from Table 3.2 again, we see that the impact coefficient for the "woman candidate" variable is -.38. This tells us that as we move from evaluations of men candidates (coded 0) to evaluations of women candidates (coded 1), evaluations become more liberal by about one-third of a point on the seven-point scale. This offers the same general information as the regression coefficients but has the benefit of evaluating all independent variables on the same scale.

Table 3.2 presents the findings for the pooled analysis of respondent perceptions of the ideology of Democratic and Republican House candidates. Taking Democrats first, the data demonstrate that respondents view a Democratic candidate as more liberal when that candidate is a woman than when the candidate is a man. This confirms the findings of previous research, both from experiments and surveys about hypothetical candidates and from analysis of actual candidates. Also relevant is the incumbency status of the woman candidate. Whereas nonincumbent Democra-

TABLE 3.2:
Determinants of Perceptions of House Candidate Ideology
Pooled Analysis 1990–2000[1]

	Democrats[2]	Republicans
Woman Candidate	-.377** (-.38)	-.095 (.10)
Party Incumbent	-.003 (.00)	.055 (.05)
Woman Incumbent	.242* (.24)	-.432* (-.43)
Ideology	-.349** (-2.09)	-.477** (-2.86)
Feeling Thermometer	-.002** (-2.14)	-.037** (-2.13)
FT*Ideology	.007** (5.45)	.009** (-3.69)
Party Ideology	.371** (2.22)	.381** (6.30)
Constant	3.242**	4.759**
N =	2629	2630
Adj. R^2 =	.33	.27

**p < .01; *p < .05

[1]This analysis does not include 1992. In that year, the NES did not ask respondents to rate the ideology of House candidates.

[2]The impact coefficient, in parentheses, gives the change in the dependent variable (ideology score) as you move from the lowest to the highest value of each independent variable, with all other variables set to their means.

tic women are viewed as more liberal, incumbent Democratic women were judged to be less liberal than challengers. This finding suggests that people do not simply take a consistent message from candidate sex and see all women candidates as more liberal (as the stereotyping literature would suggest) but instead consider candidate sex in the context of other aspects of the election, such as incumbency status. Incumbency may provide additional information to voters that offsets the cue presented by a woman candidate's sex. Voters generally have less information about challengers than incumbents, so candidate sex becomes a more valued piece of information when voters evaluate a challenger.

For evaluations of Republican candidates, the sex of the candidate is not significant to overall evaluations. Women Republicans are not perceived differently from men Republicans. However, incumbency status is again relevant to perceptions of women candidates. Here, women Republican incumbents are seen as somewhat less conservative than men Republican incumbents. This finding is in line with experimental work suggesting that people view Republican women as more moderate than Republican men and provides another example of how sex and partisan stereotypes can influence each other.

Beyond candidate sex, the analysis demonstrates the primary importance of personal and partisan attitudes to ideological evaluations. For evaluations of both Democratic and Republican candidates, perceptions of ideology are determined by a respondent's own ideology, his or her feelings about the candidates, and perceptions of the ideology of the political parties. These findings suggest that people project their own ideology onto the candidates they are evaluating, especially when they feel positively toward the candidate. In the end, partisan attitudes appear to have a much stronger impact on people's evaluations than does candidate sex. But, at least among Democratic candidates, sex stereotypes can have an impact. This would suggest that stereotypes can complement or moderate each other, depending on the party of the candidate.

The analysis of individual elections is presented in Table 3.3. For clarity of presentation, only the two major variables of interest to this analysis, sex of the candidate and the incumbency status of the woman, are included. However, the analysis indicates that the partisan variables (respondent ideology, feelings toward candidates, and perceptions of party ideology) all maintain a significant relationship to candidate ideology evaluations in all years. Recall that in the pooled analysis, women Democratic candidates were seen as more liberal than men Democrats. This impact of sex, although important, does not appear as consistently in the year-by-year analysis. In only two years, 1990 and 1998, do respondents perceive women and men Democrats differently, rating women Democrats as more liberal than men of the same party. Similar findings are evident for evaluations of Republican candidate ideology. In only two years, 1990 and 2000, is the presence of a woman candidate related to perceptions of candidate ideology. In each of those years, respondents evaluated the Republican candidate as less conservative when that candidate was a woman. But, here again, candidate sex does not appear routinely to provide a signal to respondents as to the ideology of candidates, although on occasion it does. Even though

TABLE 3.3:
Determinants of Perceptions of House Candidate Ideology
Individual Year Analysis 1990–2000[1]

	1990	1994	1996	1998	2000
Democrats					
Woman Candidate	-.502*	-.135	.183	-.690**	-.305
Woman Incumbent	.125	-.004	-.275	.503**	-.001
N =	448	660	520	460	625
Republicans					
Woman Candidate	-.858*	-.206	.290	-.158	-.796*
Woman Incumbent	-.302	-.595	-.001**	.009	.415
N =	303	685	595	554	639

**p < .01; *p .05

[1]This analysis does not include 1992. In that year, the NES did not ask respondents to rate the ideology of House candidates.

these year-to-year findings may suggest that people do not universally employ sex stereotypes when they evaluate the political views of women candidates, we must keep in mind that the pool of women candidates and the sample of respondents is more limited in the individual year samples than in the pooled analysis. Indeed, given the larger sample size and more diverse group of women candidates, the pooled analysis provides the best representation of general trends, and we should consider the individual year analyses in this light.

Salience

Another way to evaluate how the public perceives women candidates is to take a measure of how much information they possess about them. Whether or not people have sufficient levels of information about candidates is crucial to potential support. Although most House elections are relatively low-information affairs in which people don't possess significant knowledge about the candidates, it is unlikely that many people would vote for a candidate about whom they know nothing.

Previous literature does not lead us to a clear set of expectations about whether the public would be more or less likely to know more about women candidates than they know about men. There is a significant body of literature that demonstrates that the media, most people's major source of information about political candidates, tends to focus less on women candidates, or at least it provides different types of information about women candidates than about men.[26] Others might suggest that, because women are still a minority of candidates for office at every level, their distinctiveness may make them stand out, which could result in the public hearing more about them. At the same time, women candidates, who are often challengers in congressional elections, may not be any more or less visible than the average male challenger.

The NES includes a series of questions that will allow us to take a measure of whether candidate sex has an impact on the amount of information respondents have about House candidates. Respondents are asked if there is anything they like about the House candidates in their district. If a respondent answers "yes," he or she is then given up to five opportunities to list things they like. The same procedure is used to determine if there is anything a respondent dislikes about the House candidates. As with the ideology evaluation, the questions are asked separately for Democratic and Republican candidates. To determine how salient the candidates are to respondents, the number of likes and dislikes are added together to create a measure of the total amount of information mentioned about a candidate, regardless of the content of the comments.

There are a number of potential explanations that offer help in interpreting salience evaluations of candidates. First, of course, we want to determine whether people are more likely to see candidates as more salient when the candidate being evaluated is a woman. Also, because of their unique position, we need to consider whether incumbents are evaluated differently from other candidates. By virtue of being incumbents, voters will generally base evaluations on more information, regardless of content. We should also expect that members of a candidate's political party will assign higher scores, as would people who begin with more positive evaluations of that candidate. For this reason, the model includes measures of respondent political party and the feeling thermometer evaluation of each party's House candidates. Finally, we also want to consider the impact of respondent sex and education level. Past literature has raised the notion of an "affinity effect," the stronger feelings that women have toward women candidates. It may be that women are more likely to be more aware of women candidates than men. Also, because possessing information about congressional candidates requires people to pay some attention to the political world around them, we assume that people with higher levels of education should possess more information about the candidates, resulting in higher salience scores.

The analysis of the pooled data for all six elections is presented in Table 3.4. Remember that salience scores measure the total amount of information that respondents listed when asked for their likes and dislikes of each party's candidates. So what we are getting at here is how much a person can say about a candidate. Saying more about a candidate presupposes having more information about that candidate, which can be turned into evaluative statements of like and dislike. Because sex is an information cue, it could work to increase the amount of accessible information people possess.

The models for Democratic and Republican candidates are quite similar. In evaluating candidates of both parties, respondents make more comments when that candidate is a woman, although the effect is somewhat stronger for a Democratic woman. The impact coefficient for Democratic women indicates that respondents made .42 more mentions, whereas they made .26 more mentions for Republican women. This lends some support for the notion that women candidates' distinctness can make them more visible to the public and can trigger information that may not be triggered by men candidates. Incumbency status is also important to the amount of knowledge people have about candidates. It is not surprising that people would give higher scores to incumbents because the information about them is vast and more easily obtained than information about challengers. However, the incumbency status of the woman candidate is not significantly related to the amount of information people have; here sex provides incumbents with no additional benefits over the ones they already enjoy.

TABLE 3.4:
Determinants of House Candidate Salience Scores
Pooled Analysis 1990–2000

	Democrats[1]	Republicans
Woman Candidate	.392** (.42)	.267* (.26)
Party Incumbent	.398** (.39)	.452** (.45)
Woman Incumbent	-.138 (-.14)	.125 (.13)
Feeling Thermometer	.015** (1.58)	.011** (1.15)
Party Identification	-.014 (-.11)	.023* (.14)
Sex	-.178** (-.18)	-.157** (-.16)
Education	.187** (1.12)	.196** (1.18)
N =	4900	4409
Adj. R^2 =	.11	.11

**p < .01; *p .05

[1]The impact coefficient, in parentheses, gives the change in the dependent variable (number of candidate mentions) as you move from the lowest to the highest value of each independent variable, with all other variables set to their means.

The other variables in the model are related to salience scores in the ways expected. The amount of information people can articulate about candidates is a function of a couple of partisan attitudes: their feelings for the candidates (more positive feelings are associated with possessing more information) and party identification (although only when evaluating Republicans). Also, respondent sex and education level are significant. Men are more likely to hold more information about candidates than women, which confirms the findings of small, but significant, differences in political knowledge among women and men and would seem to dispute the idea that women are more likely to "notice" women candidates than are men.[27] As would be expected, respondents with higher levels of education can mention more information in making evaluations of candidates than those with lower levels of education.

TABLE 3.5:
Determinants of House Candidate Salience Scores
Individual Year Analysis 1990–2000

	1990	1992	1994	1996	1998	2000
Democrats						
Woman Candidate	.691**	.271*	-.009	.648**	-.108	.624**
Woman Incumbent	-.240	.194	.397	-.364	.008	-.559*
N =	757	1247	949	743	524	770
Republicans						
Woman Candidate	.001	.155	.205	.228	.286	.003
Woman Incumbent	-.239	.333	.826	.415	-.336	-.002
N =	456	1032	926	801	613	777

**p < .01; *p .05

As with the analysis of political ideology, an examination of the individual election years offered in Table 3.5 reveals interesting patterns in salience scores. For Democratic candidates, respondents were more likely to possess more information when the candidate was a woman in four of the six elections. Interestingly, the only time the incumbency status of the woman is related to the amount of information people have about candidates is in 2000, when respondents gave less information about the incumbent Democratic candidate when she was a woman.

In the year-by-year analysis, candidate sex is never significantly related to salience scores for Republican candidates. This would imply that respondents have no more information about Republican women than they do about Republican men. That the impact of candidate sex is fairly strong for Democratic candidates and is nonexistent for Republicans provides interesting food for thought. It may be that Republican women are inconsistent, at some level, with people's stereotyped expectations about women candidates. This inconsistency could lead to confusion rather than clarity, resulting in people's holding less information about these women.

Issue Stereotypes

The final evaluations of women candidates to be examined tap into perceived differences in policy interests and specialties between women and men. There is a significant body of research that demonstrates that the public sees women as ideally suited for such issues as education, health, welfare, and children's issues. Men are seen by many as possessing the interest, power, and temperament to address such things as military and economic issues.[28] These stereotypes as applied to candidates and politicians are thought to stem from the more general stereotypes that people apply to women and men in society. Results from experimental research caution that these stereotypes could work against women candidates if they are not seen by voters as competent to deal with the issues of the day.[29] But whether people evaluate women candidates based on these issue areas remains to be seen.

The opportunities the NES gives respondents to identify things that they like and dislike about congressional candidates also provide a way to measure what sort of issues people mention when evaluating these candidates. Many of the comments respondents make deal with a broad range of policy issues, from economic issues and the environment to defense and social policy. These comments were recoded into categories that represent the stereotypical "female" and "male" issues.[30] Aside from candidate sex and incumbency status, the analysis includes respondent political party, sex, and level of education.

As with the earlier analysis, evaluations of Democratic and Republican candidates are presented separately. If people employ issues stereotypes when evaluating women candidates, we would expect that they would mention more of these issues when the candidate being evaluated is a woman than when they are evaluating a man. Table 3.6 presents the findings for the pooled analysis of the six House elections under consideration. When respondents are evaluating Democratic House candidates, they are significantly more likely to mention stereotypical female issues

TABLE 3.6:
Determinants of Candidate Evaluations—Issue Stereotypes
Pooled Analysis 1990–2000

Democrats

	Female Issues[1]		Male Issues	
Woman Candidate	.082**	(.08)	.013	(.01)
Party Incumbent	.045**	(.05)	.056**	(.06)
Woman Incumbent	-.019	(-.02)	.006	(.01)
Party Identification	-.007**	(-.04)	-.001	(-.01)
Sex	-.001	(.00)	-.029**	(-.03)
Education	.025**	(.16)	.015**	(.09)
Constant	-.008		.028	
N =	6047		6043	
Adj R^2 =	.02		.02	

Republicans

	Female Issues		Male Issues	
Woman Candidate	.012	(.02)	.003	(.00)
Party Incumbent	.036**	(.04)	.021**	(.02)
Woman Incumbent	.007	(.01)	-.021	(-.02)
Party Identification	.002	(.01)	.007**	(.05)
Sex	.003	(.00)	-.035**	(.04)
Education	.027**	(.16)	.013**	(.08)
Constant	-.041		.004*	
N =	5575		5577	
Adj. R^2 =	.02		.02	

**p < .01; *p .05

[1]The impact coefficient, in parentheses, gives the change in the dependent variable (number of female or male issue mentions) as you move from the lowest to the highest value of each independent variable, with all other variables set to their means.

when the candidate is a woman than when the candidate is a man. This different response would support the idea that the presence of a woman candidate stimulates people to activate their stereotypes about the abilities and interests of such a candidate. It may also be the case that when a woman candidate is a Democrat, the stereotypes people hold about her interests are reinforced by partisan stereotypes, which generally assume Democrats to be more concerned about such issues as working families, the environment, and social issues. Interestingly, the incumbency status of the woman candidate is not significant, indicating that people's perceptions are driven by candidate sex, and being an incumbent does not alter this relationship.

Other significant variables conform to expectations. Democratic identifiers are more likely to mention female issues when evaluating their party's candidates than are Republican identifiers. Also, those with higher levels of education are more likely to mention female issues than those with lower levels of education. This difference is most likely a function of the overall higher levels of information associated with higher levels of education.

Interestingly, candidate sex is not significantly related to respondents' likelihood of mentioning male issues when evaluating Democrats. Stereotypes about women and men may lead us to expect that people would be significantly less likely to discuss male issues when evaluating women, but this is not the case. Instead, respondents exhibit no differences in mentioning male issues when evaluating women and men. Incumbency is related to male evaluations, which probably means that people are simply more likely to mention issues of all kinds when evaluating an incumbent. Education is significant again, with people who have higher levels of education being more likely to mention male issues when evaluating Democrats. Finally, respondent sex is significant, with men being more likely than women to mention male issues in their candidate evaluations.

The determinants of issue evaluations for Republican candidates are similar to those for Democrats with one major exception. Candidate sex is not significantly related to mentioning issues—either female or male—when people evaluate Republican candidates. So respondents are no more likely to employ female issues, or less likely to use male issues, when the Republican is a woman, a finding counter to what the stereotyping literature would suggest. Here again, the analysis points to the important interactions between candidate sex and their political party. People are more likely to employ female issue evaluations when evaluating women Democrats because the sex and party stereotypes are consistent. This situation makes it easier for people to apply the stereotypes. But for Republican women candidates, the sex and partisan cues are conflicting, which makes it difficult for people to form a clear evaluation. Here it would appear that, when signals are mixed, partisan stereotypes are more likely to shape evaluations, or at least affect sex stereotypes. As with Democratic candidates, incumbent candidates stimulate more issues, both female and male, being mentioned. Also, people with higher education are more likely to mention both types of issues more often, and men are significantly more likely to offer male issue evaluations than are women.

The individual year analysis presented in Table 3.7 demonstrates again that the impact of candidate sex in elections is not a consistent one. These data demonstrate that people are more likely to use female issues when evaluating Democratic women candidates than Democratic men, but only in three of the six election years: 1990, 1996, and 2000. Interestingly, there is no such effect for 1992, a year in which Democratic women candidates were identified with domestic and women's issues in the media to a much greater degree than usual. Respondents were actually more likely to employ male issues when the Democrat being evaluated was a woman in 1990, the only time this finding is established. Also, in 1996, respondents were significantly less likely to mention either female or male issues when the incumbent candidate being evaluated was a woman. Why this may be the case is unclear, but it does point to the idiosyncratic nature of individual election circumstances.

For Republican candidates, candidate sex is only related to mentioning female issues in one year—1996. Clearly respondents are less likely to identify Republican women with the traditional female issues than they are Democratic women in a consistent fashion, although they may in a particular election. Interestingly, in 1996, respondents are also significantly more likely to mention male issues when the Republican they are evaluating is a woman. Note also that female issues were significantly associated with evaluating women Democrats in 1996. It may be that people simply had more issue information of all types about women candidates in this year, for whatever reason, than in the others under examination.

TABLE 3.7:
Determinants of Candidate Evaluations—Issue Stereotypes
Individual Year Analysis 1990–2000

Democrats

Female Issues

	1990	1992	1994	1996	1998	2000
Woman Candidate	.161**	.002	.007	.009**	.002	.009*
Woman Incumbent	.001	.005	-.003	-.191**	.005	-.002
N =	901	1449	1139	1151	684	932

Male Issues

	1990	1992	1994	1996	1998	2000
Woman Candidate	.008*	.004	-.006	.001	-.002	.003
Woman Incumbent	-.009	.001	.003	-.120*	.001	.005
N =	901	1447	1136	1151	684	931

Republicans

Female Issues

	1990	1992	1994	1996	1998	2000
Woman Candidate	-.006	.002	-.001	.136**	.003	-.007
Woman Incumbent	.006	-.001	-.008	-.006	-.106	.008
N =	646	1287	1108	1183	761	940

Male Issues

	1990	1992	1994	1996	1998	2000
Woman Candidate	-.002	-.002	-.003	.006*	-.008	.001
Woman Incumbent	.006	-.008	-.004	-.008	-.005	-.004
N =	646	1289	1109	1183	761	940

**p < .01; *p .05

Discussion

The findings of experimental research on the impact of candidate sex strongly suggest that people think about women in a particular way, one that is governed by gender-based stereotypes. However, as has been suggested, the artificial nature of an experimental setting does not mirror actual election conditions. Experiments are able to isolate the influence of candidate sex on a respondent's evaluations, but in the real world, candidate sex is simply one piece of information among many that voters (potentially) possess. Although candidate sex may be relevant in some circumstances, it is probably impossible for the average voter to make an evaluation based on sex alone, separating out the influences of her party or even that voter's own political and ideological interests. When using data from real-world elections involving women and men candidates, we see that candidate sex is less central to the evaluations of congressional candidates on a consistent basis than previous work has led us to expect.

Analysis of the entire period under consideration demonstrates a role for candidate sex on the public's evaluation of candidates. When evaluating Democratic candidates, people are more likely to see them as liberal, to hold more information about them, and to use female issues in their evaluations when that candidate is a woman. For Republican candidates, candidate sex is much less likely to be related to how people evaluate them. People did hold more information about Republican candidates when they were women but did not evaluate candidate ideology or stereotyped issues differently for women or men candidates. However, the analysis of individual election years suggests that these relationships were not consistent across all years. In the majority of the elections examined here, candidate sex had little bearing on how liberal or conservative a candidate was thought to be. In most election years, respondents did not have appreciably more information about women candidates than they did about men. Nor was there a widespread tendency on the part of respondents to stereotype women candidates by evaluating them with an eye toward female policy issues. Instead, the analysis here would suggest that women candidates, more often than not, were assessed in a very similar fashion to men. This finding suggests that candidate sex, by itself, is not necessarily the primary influence on evaluations but instead may be interacting with other influences in the electoral environment.

One of these other influences is clearly political party. Democratic and Republican women are evaluated quite differently by respondents. Democratic women are seen as more liberal than Democratic men, but people make only limited distinctions in the political ideology of Republican women and men. People employ female issue stereotypes when evaluating Democratic women but do not use issue stereotypes when evaluating Republican women. This incongruity would suggest that political party considerations are working along with candidate sex in the minds of respondents. As stated earlier, the consistent sex and partisan cues offered by Democratic women may make it easier for people to retrieve information about these women. Republican women, however, offer conflicting cues: those based on sex, which should lead people toward ideology and issue stereotypes in a liberal/female direction, and those based on party, which would lead people toward conservative/male impressions. Because of this conflict, people may simply block out these messages or fail to use them when developing evaluations of these women candidates, pointing to the fact that candidate sex is not a simple, straightforward influence on the public's evaluations but instead can set off a fairly complex set of considerations.

Evaluations of political candidates are an important starting point for any discussion of public reaction. But the most important "evaluation" that people can make is at the ballot box with their decision about for which candidate they will vote. Whether, when, and who will vote for women candidates are still largely unanswered questions. It is to those questions that we now turn.

Notes

1. Macrae, C. Neil, Charles Stangor, and Miles Hewstone, *Stereotypes and Stereotyping* (London: Guilford Press, 1996).

2. Fiske, Susan, and Steven Neuberg, "A Continuum of Impression Formation, from Category-Based to Individuating Processes: Influences of Information and Motivation on Attention and Interpretation," in *Advances in Experimental Social Psychology*, ed. Mark Zanna (San Diego: Academic Press, 1990).

3. Ashmore, Richard, Frances Del Boca, and Arthur Wohlers, "Gender Stereotypes," in *The Social Psychology of Female-Male Relations: A Critical Analysis of Central Concepts*, ed. Richard Ashmore and Frances Del Boca (Orlando, Fla.: Academic Press, 1986); Broverman, Inge, Susan Vogel, Donald Broverman, Frank Clarkson, and Paul Rosenkrantz, "Sex Role Stereotypes: A Current Appraisal," *Journal of Social Issues* 28 (1974):59–78.

4. Williams, John, and Deborah Best, *Measuring Sex Stereotypes: A Multination Study* (Newbury Park, Calif.: Sage Publications, 1990).

5. Eagly, Alice, *Sex Differences in Social Behavior: A Social-Role Interpretation* (Hillsdale, N.J.: Erlbaum, 1987).

6. von Baeyer, Carl, Debbie Sherk, and Mark Zanna, "Impression Management in the Job Interview: When the Female Applicant Meets the Male (Chauvinist) Interviewer," *Personality and Social Psychology Bulletin* 7 (1981):45–51; Zanna, Mark, and Susan Pack, "On the Self-Fulfilling Nature of Apparent Sex Differences in Behavior," *Journal of Experimental Social Psychology* 11 (1975):583–591.

7. Alexander, Deborah, and Kristi Andersen, "Gender as a Factor in the Attribution of Leadership Traits," *Political Research Quarterly* 46 (1993):527–545; Huddy, Leonie, and Nayda Terkildsen, "Gender Stereotypes and the Perception of Male and Female Candidates," *American Journal of Political Science* 37 (1993a):119–147.

8. King, David, and Richard Matland, "Partisanship and the Impact of Candidate Gender in Congressional Elections: Results of an Experiment," paper presented at the Women Transforming Congress conference, Carl Albert Center, University of Oklahoma, 1999; McDermott, Monika, "Race and Gender Cues in Low-Information Elections," *Political Research Quarterly* 51 (1998):895–918.

9. Koch, Jeffrey, "Do Citizens Apply Gender Stereotypes to Infer Candidates' Ideological Orientations?" *Journal of Politics* 62 (2000):414–429; Koch, Jeffrey, "Gender Stereotypes and Citizens' Impression of House Candidates Ideological Orientations," *American Journal of Political Science* 46 (2002):453–462.

10. Dodson, Debra, "Acting for Women: Is What Legislators Say, What They Do?" in *The Impact of Women in Public Office*, ed. Susan Carroll (Bloomington: Indiana University Press, 2002); Frankovic, Kathleen, "Sex and Voting in the U.S. House of Representatives: 1961–1975," *American Politics Quarterly* 5 (1977):315–330; Welch, Susan, "Are Women More Liberal Than Men in the U. S. Congress?" *Legislative Studies Quarterly* 10 (1985):125–134.

11. Brown, Clyde, Neil Heighberger, and Peter Shocket, "Gender-Based Differences in Perceptions of Male and Female City Council Candidates," *Women and Politics* 13 (1993):1–17; Huddy and Terkildsen 1993a; Kahn, Kim, "Does Being Male Help? An Investigation of the Effects of Candidate Gender and Campaign Coverage on Evaluations of U.S. Senate Candidates," *Journal of Politics* 54 (1992):497–517; Leeper, Mark, "The Impact of Prejudice on Female Candidates: An Experimental Look at Voter Inference," *American Politics Quarterly* 19 (1991):248–261.

12. Williams and Best 1990.

13. Leeper 1991; Sapiro, Virginia, "If U.S. Senator Baker Were a Woman: An Experimental Study of Candidate Images," *Political Psychology* 2 (1981/82):61–83.

14. Huddy, Leonie, and Nayda Terkildsen, "The Consequences of Gender Stereotypes for Women Candidates at Different Levels and Types of Offices," *Political Research Quarterly* 46 (1993b):503–525; Rosenwasser, Shirley, and Norma Dean, "Gender Role and Political Office: Effects of Perceived Masculinity/Femininity of Candidate and Political Office," *Psychology of Women Quarterly* 13 (1989):77–85.

15. Alexander and Andersen 1993; Huddy and Terkildsen 1993a; Kahn 1992; Koch, Jeffrey, "Candidate Gender and Assessments of Senate Candidates," *Social Science Quarterly* 80 (1999):84–96; Leeper 1991.

16. Alexander and Andersen 1993; Kahn, Kim, *The Political Consequences of Being a Woman: How Stereotypes Influence the Conduct and Consequences of Political Campaigns* (New York: Columbia University Press, 1996); Koch 1999.

17. Dolan, Kathleen, "Voting for Women in the 'Year of the Woman,'" *American Journal of Political Science* 42 (1998):272–293.

18. Huddy and Terkildsen 1993a; Kahn 1996.

19. Dolan 1998; Paolino, Philip, "Group-Salient Issues and Group Representation: Support for Women Candidates in the 1992 Senate Elections," *American Journal of Political Science* 39 (1995):294–313; Plutzer, Eric, and John Zipp, "Identity Politics, Partisanship, and Voting for Women Candidates," *Public Opinion Quarterly* 60 (1996):30–57.

20. Rahn, Wendy, "The Role of Partisan Stereotypes in Information Processing About Political Candidates," *American Journal of Political Science* 37 (1993):472–496.

21. Center for American Women and Politics (CAWP), *Fact Sheet*, "Women Candidates for Congress 1974–2000: Party and Seat Summary for Major Party Nominees" (New Brunswick, N.J.: Eagleton Institute of Politics, Rutgers University, 2000).

22. Huddy, Leonie, and Teresa Capelos, "Gender Stereotyping and Candidate Evaluation: Good News and Bad News for Women Politicians," in *The Social Psychology of Politics*, ed. Victor Ottati et al. (New York: Kluwer Academic Press, 2002).

23. The full scale runs as follows: 1 = extremely liberal; 2 = liberal; 3 = slightly liberal; 4 = moderate, middle of the road; 5 = slightly conservative; 6 = conservative; 7 = extremely conservative.

24. Conover, Pamela, and Stanley Feldman, "Candidate Perception in an Ambiguous World," *American Journal of Political Science* 33 (1989):912–939; Koch 2000; Krosnik, Jon, "Americans' Perceptions of Presidential Candidates: A Test of the Projection Hypothesis," *Journal of Social Issues* 46 (1990):159–182.

25. The one exception to this is the analysis of political ideology. Data for 1992 are not available because the NES did not ask respondents to rate the ideology of House candidates that year.

26. Kahn 1996.

27. Delli Carpini, Michael, and Scott Keeter, *What Americans Know About Politics and Why It Matters* (New Haven: Yale University Press, 1996).

28. Alexander and Andersen 1993; Brown, Heighberger, and Shocket 1993; Leeper 1991; Sapiro 1981/82.

29. Huddy and Terkildsen 1993a.

30. Female issues include education, welfare, health, Social Security, civil rights, abortion, women's rights, day care, family leave, and the environment. Male issues include economic issues, taxes, monetary policy, employment policies, crime, drugs, military, and international issues.

4

Who Votes for
Women Candidates?
Voter Demographics

RECALL THAT CHAPTER 1 suggests that there are several reasons why voters might choose (or fail to choose) to vote for a woman candidate. Following Hanna Pitkin's formulation of the concept of representation, voters may choose women (or any) candidates because they seek descriptive ("standing for") or substantive ("acting for") representation. The first of these, descriptive representation, focuses attention on the demographic characteristics of both voters and candidates for office. This relationship can encompass a number of considerations: race, ethnicity, sex, religion, and even age. Voters who seek to elect "one of their own" to office are motivated by a belief, either implicit or explicit, that candidates who share their personal characteristics will represent that group in office. At its most basic level, descriptive representation can be important to voters who don't see enough people like them in office and want the picture of government to reflect people like themselves. Correcting this underrepresentation can be a legitimate expression of the desire to change the face of government. And yet voting on the basis of descriptive representation is not exclusively carried out by voters who choose candidates with whom they share traits. Indeed, white voters can value racial diversity and seek out candidates who represent racial minorities, and men can vote for women candidates to increase the sex balance of elected offices.

A consideration of voting based on demographic traits causes us to ask the question, "Who votes for women candidates?" Are there certain types of people who are more or less likely to support women? Can we use race, sex, religion, or other variables to identify those who might be most sympathetic to women candidates? These questions will be the focus of this chapter.

Influences on Congressional Vote Choice

Before we can determine which, if any, demographic characteristics are related to choosing to vote for women candidates, we must first understand the role these factors play in the general voting decision. In searching for clues as to how voters make up their minds about which candidates to support, researchers have usually found that the role of demographic factors is somewhat limited. Instead, three variables are seen as most directly linked to an individual's vote choice: political party identification, candidate images, and issues.[1] Further, because we are examining congressional elections in this analysis, we must consider the impact of incumbency on vote choice.

Since the earliest studies of voting behavior in the United States, political party identification has been recognized as having the most significant impact on shaping vote choice. Political party identification has long been seen by political scientists as an attachment or loyalty to one of the major political parties that is acquired early in life and that acts to shape a person's vote choice and political behavior in the future.[2] It is considered to be a long-term influence, based on long-standing attitudes about political phenomena, and is, for most people, relatively stable. Voters use party identification as a shortcut in making their voting decisions. Because relatively little information is (easily) available to the average voter, party identification becomes important in helping voters to identify which candidate most closely matches their political views. Indeed, most Americans claim an identification with a political party, if only a weak one, with the vast majority of them aligning themselves with the Democratic or Republican parties.[3] Third parties in the United States have relatively few adherents.[4] To support the primacy of party identification to vote choice, scholars demonstrate that, for as long as we have been able to collect data on these issues, most Republican identifiers vote for Republican candidates, and most Democrats vote for Democrats. For example, in 2000, 83 percent of Democrats voted for Al Gore for president, and 89 percent of Republicans voted for George W. Bush. This general pattern has held true, with some deviation in particular years, since 1952.[5]

The primacy of political party identification is demonstrated again through its relationship to the other major influences on vote choice: candidate image and issues. It should not be surprising that people's evaluations of candidates and their positions on issues are influenced by their political party connections. So although it is clear that voters overwhelmingly vote for the candidate they rate most highly and usually vote for the candidates with whom they agree on the issues, it is also true that these actions tend to cause voters to end up choosing the candidate of their own political party. Of course, this relationship is not perfect because some Democrats vote for Republican candidates and vice versa. But, in general, these three influences are intertwined and provide the strongest relationship to vote choice.

In this analysis, we must also account for the impact of incumbency. Most scholars of congressional elections agree that incumbency is the single most important aspect of congressional elections. Incumbent members of Congress have a multitude of resources at their disposal when they campaign for reelection, which often leaves the candidates who are challenging with little way to attract attention.[6] Senate challengers, who tend to be more experienced, usually fare somewhat better than House challengers, who are often all but invisible to the public. Incumbent members in both chambers have higher name recognition among the public than challengers and also tend to have fairly high public approval ratings, an average of 83 percent approval rating for House incumbents in 2000.[7] Incumbent reelection rates, averaging 90 percent or better for both members of the House and Senate, speak to the power of incumbency as a factor in vote choice.[8]

Many observers see incumbency as one of the primary roadblocks standing in the way of women's integration into Congress. Incumbent members of Congress are overwhelmingly male, which means that women candidates are more often in the unenviable position of running as challengers or perhaps as open-seat candidates. In the six elections from 1990 to 2000, there were 650 women candidates for the House and 53 for the Senate. Of those who ran for the House, 47 percent did so as challengers, and another 17 percent were candidates for open seats. Fully 51 percent of the women candidates for the Senate ran as challengers, with another 28 percent running for open seats. Given that challenging candidates, whether female or male, are overwhelmingly unlikely to win, having almost half of all women candidates running as challengers helps explain the slow movement of women into Congress.[9]

Demographic Influences on Vote Choice

What, then, is the impact of demographic variables such as race, sex, and income? These factors can be important in shaping a person's vote choice, but they are a secondary set of influences. According to one viewpoint, there is only an "indirect relationship between group membership and the vote."[10] Indeed, even though popular presentations of politics often refer to the "soccer moms" or the "senior citizens vote," most researchers caution us about making too much of the influence of any one demographic variable taken alone. For example, looking at the "senior vote" envisions a bloc of older voters whose choices are driven by considerations related to their age. But among any group of older voters, some are women and some are men; some are wealthy whereas others are poor; and some are black, white, Hispanic, Asian, and so forth. When political scientists do focus on demographic characteristics, they generally do so as these variables relate to partisan identification. Higher socioeconomic people—the well-educated, white, high-income people—are more likely to vote Republican, whereas poorer people—those with less education and racial minorities—are more likely to vote for Democratic candidates. So, even though patterns of voting activity among any particular group of people can often be demonstrated, the relationship is more closely related to shared party identification than to demographic group identities.

Demographic Influences on Voting for Women Candidates

The obvious question to ask when examining the impact of voter demographics on voting for women candidates is "Do women vote for women?" This so-called "affinity effect" has been an implicit, and sometimes explicit, assumption underlying much of the research done on women candidates. Past research indicates several reasons for the assumption that women voters will be more likely to vote for women candidates than men will. First, some expect that a sense of group identity will draw women voters to women candidates. Indeed, several experimental studies demonstrate that voters are most likely to choose candidates like themselves. For example, black voters are more likely to choose black candidates than are whites.[11] Other researchers refer to the impact of a "gender consciousness" at work, suggesting that women voters have positive feelings toward women candidates beyond a simple shared demographic similarity. Here these positive feelings toward women candidates "as women" are shaped, perhaps, by an acknowledgment of the underrepresentation of women in elected office or a sense that women's political fortunes are bound up with other women.[12] Important as well is the role of political issues in the relationship between women voters and women candidates. It is possible that there are "group-salient" issues that draw women voters to women candidates. Such issues as sexual harassment, abortion, or child care tend to be of greater importance to women voters, and women voters may see women candidates as uniquely suited to dealing with these issues.[13] Finally, a link between women voters and women candidates may not be based on gender or gender-based issues per se but instead on a shared partisan identity. Currently, women in the United States are more likely to identify with the Democratic Party than the Republican Party, and more women candidates run for office as Democrats than as Republicans. Women voters, who are more likely to be Democrats, may simply be choosing candidates of their party, many of whom are women.[14]

In a recent article, Kira Sanbonmatsu argues that people have a baseline gender preference for either female or male candidates and that this preference is a standing predisposition, not an evaluation made on the spot during a particular election.[15] Using an experimental design and hypothetical candidates, she demonstrates that many people do have a baseline preference for voting for candidates of a particular sex, which provides support for the idea that voters take the sex of a candidate into account when making their voting decision. In her sample, Sanbonmatsu finds that women are more likely to express a preference for candidates of a certain sex than were men and that they were more likely to prefer women.[16] This finding has been supported by numerous other studies, whether they involve women simply preferring women candidates in some hypothetical situation or voting for them in an actual election.[17]

Yet at the same time, there is significant evidence to suggest that it is overly simplistic to say that women vote for women. Women voters do not always vote for women candidates, and some never do. Instead, women may be more likely to choose women candidates than men voters would be, but this dynamic is often shaped by other factors, such as race, political party, and level of office. For example, studies have demonstrated that certain subgroups of women—African Americans; liberal, feminist, and well-educated women—are more likely to choose women candidates than are other women.[18] Other work has shown that women voters may be influenced by the level of office involved, being more likely to choose women candidates for the House of Representatives, but no more likely than men to do so in Senate elections, and that Democratic women candidates often do much better in garnering votes from women than do Republican women.[19]

So even though the sex of a voter can be an important influence on the choice to support a woman candidate, it is not necessarily the only, or most important, one. Women candidates still present the public with a somewhat nontraditional political decision, and it is therefore appropriate to examine whether other personal characteristics are relevant to vote choice. If certain types of people are more or less likely to support women candidates, demonstrating these dynamics can help us better understand the challenges and opportunities that women candidates face. Moving beyond voter sex, I consider the influence of race, education, religiosity, and age. In a similar manner to women's support for women candidates, voters from racial minority groups may be more likely to choose women candidates than white voters because of their experiences as members of groups currently underrepresented in elective office.[20] Education level may be important to support for women candidates because those with higher levels of education are often more accepting of nontraditional approaches and may have more egalitarian attitudes about the appropriate roles for women and men in society. Because more religious people tend to have more traditional social values, religiosity could also have an influence on vote choice in a race involving a woman candidate. Finally, age may play a significant role in shaping vote choice regarding women candidates. Older voters, socialized in a time when women's roles were more constrained, may still see politics as an inappropriate place for women. On the other hand, younger voters may not have these same views about women in politics and may be more likely to show support for women candidates.[21]

In sum, it is important to consider characteristics of the voter that may have an impact on women candidates. Women candidates are not "invisible" to the public: Their sex is obvious, and their difference from the expected norm of the traditional male candidate is as well. Women candidates are also not evaluated by the public in isolation. Each voter examines a candidate through the lens of his or her own attributes and experiences. Whether these attributes and experiences can pull people toward women candidates or push them away is an important question.

A First Look at Support for Women—
The General Social Survey

One place to begin an examination of the impact of voter demographic characteristics on support for women candidates is the General Social Survey (GSS). Since 1972, the GSS has asked survey respondents whether they would support a woman candidate for president. The question used in the survey is this: "If your party nominated a woman for President, would you vote for her if she were qualified for the job?" This question, and its replication in most annual surveys since 1972, allows us to track the public's response to this hypothetical situation over time. Recall that in 1972, 74 percent of respondents indicated that they would support a woman presidential candidate from their party. By 1998, 94 percent said that they would vote for a woman candidate. Because the GSS collects demographic information on respondents, these data can also be used to construct a model that tests whether there are demographic variables significantly linked to the likelihood of supporting a woman candidate for president. The analysis presented here examines the impact of respondent sex, race, age, education level, and level of religiosity on an individual's likelihood of choosing a woman candidate in this situation. It also controls for the respondents' political party identification and political ideology, two major influences on vote choice. Also, because the GSS data cover a nearly 30-year period, a measure that accounts for the year in which the survey was taken is included. This allows for an examination of whether the trend in support for a hypothetical woman has increased or decreased over time. Finally, because the relationship of voter sex to support for a woman candidate occupies a place of primacy in the literature, a variable that considers whether the impact of voter sex has changed over time is included as well.

Table 4.1 presents the analysis of the demographic variables and their relationship to expressing support for a hypothetical woman presidential candidate. Several personal characteristics are significantly associated with support for a woman candidate, including sex, age, education level, and religiosity. In the GSS sample from 1972 to 1998, younger people, those with higher levels of education, and those with lower levels of religiosity are all more likely to say they would support a woman candidate for president. This fact, of course, means that older people, those with less education, and more religious people are less likely to vote for the woman. These findings conform to the expectations outlined earlier. Two other variables are significant: political party identification and political ideology. Here, Democrats and self-described liberals are more likely to support the woman candidate than Republicans and self-described conservatives. Again, these findings conform to our expectations. The variable measuring the year of the survey is signifi-

TABLE 4.1:
Demographic Determinants of Support for a Woman Candidate for President
General Social Survey 1972–1998
(Logistic Regression Coefficients)

	b	se(B)
Sex	-31.629**	11.836
Race	.061	.055
Age	.023**	.001
Education	-.134**	.007
Religiosity	.082**	.008
Party Identification	.069**	.011
Political Ideology	.154**	.017
Year	-.026**	.009
Sex* Year	-.016**	.005
Constant	-47.727*	19.430
N =	20,232	
Chi Square =	1,634.96	

**p < .01; *p < .05

Source: General Social Survey Cumulative File, 1972–2000

cant, which indicates that support for women from survey respondents has been steadily increasing over time. Finally, the relationship between sex of the respondent and support for women candidates is captured by both the coefficient for sex (-31.63) and the coefficient for the interaction between survey year and respondent sex (.016).

The interaction term that accounts for whether the impact of voter sex has changed over time is significant, indicating that even though women are more likely to voice support for women candidates than men over the course of the survey, the gap between women and men has been increasing over time as well. Figure 4.1 presents a visual interpretation of this, charting the impact of sex of the respondent over the 28-year period of the GSS. From this figure it is clear that the importance of sex has increased steadily, going from slightly negative or near zero in the early 1970s to a much stronger, positive relationship by the late 1990s. So although support for women candidates has been growing over time, it has grown more among women than men, resulting in a widening gender gap.

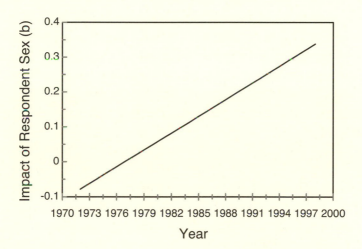

Figure 4.1: Growth in the Impact of Sex on Willingness to Vote for a Hypothetical Female Presidential Candidate 1972–1998

Examining Real-World Elections:
The National Election Study

One thing to keep in mind in reviewing the GSS data is that support for women candidates is measured by a question that asks people about a hypothetical election situation. Because the United States has never had a major party woman candidate for president, we don't really know how people would react to such a candidacy. So even though the GSS data provide a good place to begin our examination, they don't tell us the whole story. To really understand whether some types of people are more likely to support women candidates, we need to look at the actions of voters who could choose women candidates in actual elections. For that we turn to the data from the National Election Study (NES). The same demographic variables—voter sex, race, age, education, religiosity, political party, and ideology—are available in the NES. But here we are examining the behaviors of only those voters who lived in a congressional district or state in which a woman was running against a man for the House of Representatives or the Senate.[22] The dependent variable, whether a respondent voted for a female candidate or her male opponent, is not a reaction to some hypothetical situation but rather the actual vote cast by the voter in the election. When confronted with a choice between a woman and a man, which voters choose the woman?

The NES model is slightly different from the one used with the GSS data. Because the NES data are from actual election situations and not hypotheticals, there are other important political influences that we can consider. In addition to the influences on vote choice discussed so far, we can add two things. First, we can determine whether the woman candidate being considered by a voter is an incumbent or not. Incumbency has a significant impact on vote choice in congressional elections, particularly in House elections, with voters being much more likely to choose the incumbent candidate when there is one running. The advantages of incumbency are significant: extensive media exposure, generous travel and communications budgets, staff support, and high levels of name recognition. All of these translate into a situation in which well over 90 percent of incumbents who run for reelection are returned to office.[23]

Second, we know that party identification is central to vote choice. But when evaluating voting for a woman candidate, party identification can operate in two different ways. It may be the case that members of one political party are more likely to support women candidates. It would not be outrageous to suggest, for example, that Democrats, because of their assumed liberalism and commitment to equality, would be more likely to vote for women than Republicans would. However, given the strength of party identification in structuring vote choice, it would be naive to think that most Democrats would cast aside partisan loyalties and vote for a Republican woman candidate. Similarly, it would be foolish to assume that Republicans would choose a Democratic male candidate simply to avoid voting for a woman. Instead of the members of one party being more likely to vote for a woman than members of the other, it is much more likely that the vast majority of people are more likely to choose a candidate of their own party, regardless of that candidate's sex.

For this reason, two separate measures of party identification are used in this analysis. The first, party identification, is the traditional seven-point measure of party identification that determines whether people see themselves as Republicans, Democrats, or Independents. The second, party correspondence, measures the degree of correspondence in party identification between the respondent and the woman candidate in that district or state. This approach allows us to ascertain whether Democrats are more likely to support women candidates than Republicans are while controlling for the expected influence of party identification—that people vote for the candidate of their own party.

In an effort to determine if individual demographic characteristics are related to voting for a woman, a model was created and analyzed for all House and Senate elections from 1990 to 2000. Data for the six House elections in this time period were pooled together, as were the data for the six Senate elections. Readers should note that the analysis for this chapter, as well as that in Chapters 5 and 6, employs logistic regression instead of the OLS regression described in the previous chapter. Logistic regression is appropriate for analysis with a dichotomous dependent variable (a variable that takes one of only two possible values). Chapters 4 through 6 all use the same dependent variable, which is whether the respondent voted for the woman candidate (1) or not (0). The same general ideas regarding direction and significance discussed in Chapter 3 apply here. However, interpretation of the impact coefficient is slightly different. Here, the impact coefficient gives the change in the probability of voting for the woman candidate as you move from the lowest to highest value on the independent variables. Taking an example from Table 4.2, the impact coefficient for the "woman incumbent" variable for the House of Representatives is .46. This indicates that respondents are 46 percent more likely to vote for the woman candidate than the man if the woman is an incumbent, all else held constant.

Table 4.2 presents the analysis for both the House and Senate. The first thing to note is the importance of the variables that measure the incumbency status of the woman candidate and the shared party identification of the woman and the survey respondent. In both House and Senate elections, the incumbency status of the woman is significant, although the effect is stronger for House incumbents. When running for Congress, women candidates gain an advantage among voters when they are the incumbent. Clearly, incumbency is as important for women candidates as it is for men—voters are overwhelmingly likely to choose an incumbent candidate, regardless of sex. Also, with regard to party identification, the variable measuring voter/candidate party correspondence is significantly related to choosing a woman. There is no evidence here that members of one political party or the other are more likely to support women candidates. Instead, the hypothesis that people are more likely to vote for a woman candidate when they share her party affiliation is borne out. As with incumbency, what we know to be true about the influence of party does not appear to be affected by candidate sex.

Aside from the fact that each of these variables is significantly related to voting for a woman, we should take note of the strength of the relationship. In elections for each chamber, incumbency and the variable measuring shared party identification between the respondent and the woman candidate exert the strongest influence on vote choice. This finding is what we would expect for races that didn't include a woman, so we can again say that the fundamental influences on vote choice are not disturbed by the presence of a woman on the ballot.

With regard to other respondent characteristics, the results diverge a bit. Political ideology is significantly related to voting for a woman in Senate elections. Here, not surprisingly, people who espouse a more liberal ideol-

TABLE 4.2:
Demographic Determinants of Support for Women Candidates for Congress
National Election Study 1990–2000 Pooled Analysis
(Logistic Regression Coefficients)

	House of Representatives[1]		Senate	
Woman Incumbent	1.015**	(.46)	.290**	(.14)
Party Identification	.002	(.00)	-.032	(-.04)
Shared Party	2.710**	(.58)	2.657**	(.58)
Ideology	-.072	(-.11)	-.130*	(-.19)
Sex	.376*	(.09)	-.111	(-.03)
Age	-.001	(-.02)	.012*	(.21)
Education	-.012	(-.02)	.022	(.03)
Race	-.741**	(-.17)	-.526*	(-.13)
Religiosity	.083	(.08)	.054	(.05)
Year = 1990	-.484	(-.12)	-1.566**	(-.35)
Year = 1994	-.561*	(-.14)	-.647**	(-.16)
Year = 1996	-.208	(-.05)	-.164	(-.04)
Year = 2000	-.390	(-.10)	-.170	(.04)
Constant	-.617		-.704	
N =	1054		1204	
Chi Square =	510.550		531.60	
PRE =	57.70		61.50	

*p < .05; **p < .01

[1]The impact coefficient, in parentheses, gives the change in the probability of voting for the woman candidate as you move from the lowest to the highest value on the independent variable, with all other variables set to their means.

ogy are more likely to choose the woman. In House races, voter sex is significant to vote choice, with women voters being more likely than men to choose woman candidates. Based on the impact coefficient, women respondents are 9 percent more likely to vote for women than are men voters, all else held equal. This information supports the rather significant body of literature that points to an "affinity effect." Beyond this, the only other significant demographic variable is race: As hypothesized, minority voters are 17 percent more likely to vote for women candidates than are white voters (see impact coefficient). Interestingly, different variables are important for Senate races. During the period under study, women and minorities were no more likely than men or whites to choose women candidates for the Senate, but older voters were significantly more likely to do so than others.

One final set of variables to consider in this analysis is a series of variables that account for the individual years included together in the pooled analysis. Because elections are unique events, we need to determine whether there is any impact on support for women candidates that is related to a particular election year. A series of dummy variables were created to account for each election year included in the pooled data set. The year 1992 is the excluded category. As the year variables in Table 4.2 demonstrate, there are indeed significant influences on support for women candidates that result from the particular elections themselves. For House races, each of the year variables is significant and negative. This means that, relative to 1992, respondents exhibited a lesser likelihood of voting for women candidates in each of the other elections. The elections of 1990 and 1994 were the most difficult for women candidates, followed by 1996 and 2000. For Senate races, respondents in 1990 and 1994 were less likely to vote for women candidates than respondents in other years. This finding raises questions about possible differences across elections that could account for differing levels of support for women candidates. These questions will be considered in Chapter 6.

Another way to examine the relationship between voter characteristics and voting for a woman is to graph them visually. In this manner, it is easier to see the relative contribution that each individual variable makes to the overall decision to support a woman. Compared to the performance of incumbency and shared party identification, the demographic variables exert relatively little influence on voting for a woman candidate for either the House or the Senate. These relationships are made clear in Figures 4.2 (House) and 4.3 (Senate). Each figure takes the variables significant to predicting support for a woman candidate and presents their relative impact in graphic form. All other variables are set to their mean. What the bars in each cell present is the difference in probability of a respondent voting for a woman candidate under certain conditions. Take, for example, Figure 4.2, which deals with House races. The upper left cell presents the impact of a shared party identification

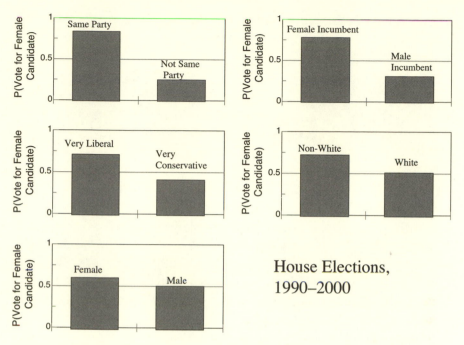

Figure 4.2: Relative Impact of Significant Variables from the Demographic Model for House Elections

between the respondent and the woman candidate. The probability that a respondent will choose the woman candidate when she is of the same party is .84, and the probability that she will be chosen when she is a member of the other party is .25. Obviously, people are overwhelmingly likely to vote for candidates of their own party, regardless of sex. Incumbency (upper right cell) exhibits the same strong effect. When the woman candidate is the incumbent, the probability that a respondent will choose her is .78, but it is only .31, less than half as likely, when her male opponent is the incumbent. Compared to these two, the influence of the other significant variables—ideology, sex, and race—are more limited.[24] Interestingly, given the findings for an affinity effect in the literature based on hypotheticals and experiments, the impact of respondent sex is the smallest of any of the significant variables. So whereas women are more likely to vote for women candidates than are men, the difference in likelihood is not dramatic.

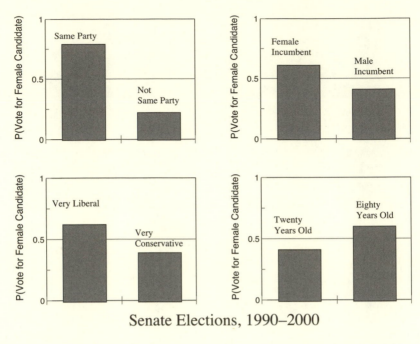

Senate Elections, 1990–2000

Figure 4.3: Relative Impact of Significant Variables from the Demographic Model for Senate Elections

The results for the Senate races are very similar. Here, there are four significant variables: shared party, incumbency, ideology, and age. For shared party, the probability of choosing the woman when she is from the respondent's party is .79, but it is only .22 if she is of the opposing party. For women incumbents, there is a .61 likelihood that they will capture the vote, but there is only a .41 likelihood if their male opponent is the incumbent. Note that Senate incumbents enjoy a somewhat smaller advantage than do House incumbents. This result is consistent with research on the differences between House and Senate elections, where Senate challengers tend to be of higher quality and are better able to give incumbents a reasonable contest.[25] As with the House races, shared party and incumbency exhibit the same strong, primary influence. Again, comparatively, the impact of ideology and age, although significant, is lesser.[26]

Individual Election Years

The analysis in Table 4.2 is important for allowing us to get an overall sense of who is most likely to vote for a woman candidate across election contests. And certainly the pooled analysis gives us the best general picture of demographic influences on support for women candidates. But we don't necessarily know if the same variables are relevant in any given election year. We should not lose sight of the fact that individual congressional elections may be influenced by different factors. Each congressional election is a unique combination of candidates, issues, voters, and local and national dynamics that can't be captured in a pooled analysis. So another way to approach the question of who is most likely to support women candidates is to examine the elections of each year separately. In this way, we can better identify which demographics represent a consistent influence on voting for a woman and which may have a more limited relationship to supporting women.

Tables 4.3 (House) and 4.4 (Senate) present the analysis for each of the six elections that took place during the time period under study. One thing to bear in mind when evaluating these findings is that the samples of both respondents and candidates is relatively small in some years, thus no doubt making it difficult to achieve statistical significance. The first patterns that emerge are similar to those demonstrated in the pooled analysis. Here again, shared party identification and the incumbency status of the woman candidate are key influences. In 11 of the 12 elections (with the exception of the Senate elections of 2000), incumbency was a significant influence. In each of the 12 elections, the party correspondence variable is the most important in the model, with voters of either party being overwhelmingly likely to choose the woman when she is a candidate of their party.

Turning to the individual demographic characteristics of voters, we see that these variables have no clear pattern of influence on voting for women. In fact, what is most striking about the information in Tables 4.3 and 4.4 is the absence of any consistent impact of voter demographics. This year-by-year analysis is instructive in establishing that the significant variables from the pooled analysis in Table 4.2 do not demonstrate a steady or stable influence on vote choice involving a woman candidate over time. Indeed, in five

TABLE 4.3:
Demographic Determinants of Support for Women Candidates for U.S. House
National Election Study 1990–2000 Individual Year Analysis
(Logistic Regression Coefficients)

	1990	1992	1994	1996	1998	2000
Woman Incumbent	1.977**	1.368**	.868*	1.132**	2.449**	2.167**
Party Identification	-.194	.123	.272*	.122	-.125	-.229#
Shared Party	2.337*	2.635**	3.539**	3.197**	3.070**	2.309**
Ideology	-.508	-.356*	-.442*	-.205	.257	.052
Sex	.104	.934*	.553	-.024	.401	.144
Age	-.023	.029*	.002	-.020	-.038*	.008
Education	.132	-.041	-.047	-.115	-.028	-.051
Race	-7.392	-1.031	-1.824*	-.668	-.254	-.278
Religiosity	-.040	.356*	.313	-.211	-.239	.013
Constant	9.179	-2.039	-.824	1.974	-.107	-1.232
N =	82	244	178	238	145	167
Chi Square =	55.608	136.898	80.868	130.524	75.515	77.007
PRE =	56.250	34.246	33.333	51.807	32.558	16.666

**p < .01; *p < .05; #p < .10

of the 12 elections for House and Senate, there are no characteristics that distinguish those who choose women candidates from those who don't, other than incumbency and shared partisanship.[27] In three years, there is a limited impact for demographics. In 1998, younger voters were more likely to choose women candidates in races for the House of Representatives than were older voters. In 2000 House races, Democrats were more likely than Republicans to do so, above and beyond the impact of the variable measuring voter/candidate party correspondence. In races for the Senate in 2000, older voters and minority voters were more likely to vote for women than younger voters and white voters.

1992 and 1994

In only two years, 1992 and 1994, is there significant evidence that voter demographics had an impact on vote choice. In 1992, the so-called "Year

TABLE 4.4:
Demographic Determinants of Support for Women Candidates for U.S. Senate National Election Study 1990–2000 Individual Year Analysis (Logistic Regression Coefficients)

	1990	1992	1994	1996	1998	2000
Woman Incumbent	1.329*	.546*	.485*	2.388*	3.054*	.499
Party Identification	.092	-.448*	-.111	.143	.106	.074
Shared Party	1.466*	.127	3.257**	1.841*	5.021**	3.627**
Ideology	.159	-.400*	-.048	.538	-.441	-.206
Sex	.114	.233	-.790*	-.929	-1.054	.405
Age	.024	.004	.023*	-.034	.031	.031*
Education	.041	.027	.078	-.211	-.035	.059
Race	-.032	-1.047*	.962	.225	.786	-1.144*
Religiosity	.064	.154	-.099	.552	-.562	.095
Constant	-3.635	3.101*	-1.341	.207	-3.072	-2.476#
N =	139	367	235	73	121	269
Chi Square =	21.398	159.150	114.276	34.376	107.199	155.356
PRE =		39.160	53.763	46.153	77.083	55.555

*p < .05; **p < .01

of the Woman," women, liberals, older voters, and less religious voters were all more likely to vote for women House candidates. In Senate races that year, Democrats, liberals, and minority voters were more likely than other voters to do so. These results largely conform to our expectations about how demographics could influence support for a woman candidate. In 1994, there are several unexpected findings. In House races, an odd coalition of Republicans, liberal voters, and racial minorities distinguish themselves in voting for women candidates. In Senate elections, men and older voters are more likely than women and younger people to do so.

Interestingly, the findings for the races in each of these election years seem to mirror the national trends in congressional elections during those campaigns. In 1992, because of their increased numbers and because of the prominence of gendered issues, such as child care and sexual harassment, women candidates had extremely high visibility and were thought to have energized women voters and others who sought to increase the number of women in Congress. The year 1994, on the other hand, was when the Republican party took control of both chambers of Congress. Here, Republican voters and male voters (who tend to be more Republican than women) were more likely to choose women candidates. The number of women serving in the House of Representatives did not change much between 1992 and 1994, going from a total of 54 after 1992 to 57 after 1994, but the specific women who were serving did. As a result of the 1994 elections, there were four fewer Democratic women and seven more Republican women than in the previous Congress.[28] In that year, the tide in favor of the Republican party served to advantage Republican women candidates.[29]

•   •   •

The results from 1992 and 1994 also raise another aspect of general support for women candidates. Data for these elections across a ten-year period demonstrate relatively inconsistent results. Each year is different from the others in the influences on voting for a woman candidate, with 1992 and 1994 standing out from the others as most distinctive. This outcome relates, in part, to an argument that support for women candidates is tied to the circumstances and the context of a particular electoral environment. This argument about how the electoral environment can help or hinder women candidates will be raised in Chapter 6.

What the findings in Tables 4.3 and 4.4 suggest is that there are very few demographic characteristics that make voters regularly more or less likely to choose women candidates in these elections. There are no clear patterns of support; there is not one major demographic influence that is always, or even often, associated with support for women candidates. In fact, the opposite is the case: The data suggest that there are idiosyncratic, election-bound influences that fail to exert any kind of systematic influence on people's evaluations of women candidates. Perhaps most significant for a discussion of demographic influences is the almost complete lack of support for the affinity effect. In only one election out of 12 (the 1992 House races) were women voters more likely than men to choose a woman candidate. There are as many occurrences (one, the House races in 1994) in which men are more likely than women to choose the woman candidate.

In the vast majority of these races, voter sex is not related to vote choice at all, although the coefficient for respondent sex is in the anticipated direction in eight of the 12 elections. This finding, based on actual election results, runs counter to several other studies, often based on experimental designs, that demonstrate an affinity effect.[30] However, before we dismiss the presence of an affinity effect, we must remember that the small sample sizes in each individual election year should cause us to interpret these results with some caution.

Instead of a dramatic impact for demographic characteristics, what we see is that the impact of two of the major influences on vote choice, incumbency and party identification, is not related to candidate sex. Women candidates in these elections are reaping the benefits of incumbency and vote support from party identifiers in the same way that those benefits have always gone to men candidates. The next step in learning more about when and why people choose women candidates is to move beyond voter characteristics to examine the political issues important to voters. As much past research suggests, it may be the case that women candidates focus on a particular set of issues in their campaigns, which can then stimulate voters who value those issues to identify that their interests will be best represented by women candidates. It is this evaluation of the role of issues in voting for women to which we now turn.

Notes

1. Luttbeg, Norman, and Michael Gant, *American Electoral Behavior: 1952–1992* (Itasca, Ill.: Peacock Publishers, 1995).

2. Campbell, Angus, Philip Converse, Warren Miller, and Donald Stokes, *The American Voter* (Ann Arbor: University of Michigan Press, 1960).

3. Abramson, Paul, John Aldrich, and David Rohde, *Change and Continuity in the 2000 Elections* (Washington, D.C.: CQ Press, 2002).

4. Ibid., p. 169.

5. Ibid., p. 177.

6. Herrnson, Paul, *Congressional Elections: Campaigning at Home and in Washington*, 3rd ed. (Washington, D.C.: CQ Press, 2000).

7. Abramson, Aldrich, and Rohde 2002.

8. Jacobson, Gary, *The Politics of Congressional Elections*, 5th ed. (New York: Longman, 2001).

9. Center for American Women and Politics (CAWP), *Fact Sheet*, "Women Candidates for Congress 1974–2000" (New Brunswick, N.J.: Eagleton Institute of Politics, Rutgers University, 2000).

10. Ibid., p. 121. See also Flanigan, William, and Nancy Zingale, *Political Behavior of the American Electorate*, 10th ed. (Washington, D.C.: CQ Press, 2002).

11. Sigelman, Lee, and Carol Sigelman, "Sexism, Racism, and Ageism in Voting Behavior: An Experimental Analysis," *Social Psychology Quarterly* 45 (1982):263–269; Sigelman, Lee, and Susan Welch, "Race, Gender, and Opinion Toward Black and Female Candidates," *Public Opinion Quarterly* 48 (1984):467–475.

12. See, for example, Rinehart, Sue Tolleson, *Gender Consciousness and Politics* (New York: Routledge, 1992).

13. Paolino, Phillip, "Group-Salient Issues and Group Representation: Support for Women Candidates in the 1992 Senate Elections," *American Journal of Political Science* 39 (1995):294–313.

14. Cook, Elizabeth, "Voter Responses to Women Senate Candidates," in *The Year of the Woman: Myths and Realities*, Eds. Elizabeth Adell Cook, Sue Thomas, and Clyde Wilcox (Boulder: Westview Press, 1994).

15. Sanbonmatsu, Kira, "Gender Stereotypes and Vote Choice," *American Journal of Political Science* 46 (2002):20–34.

16. Sanbonmatsu asks survey respondents the following question: "If two equally qualified candidates were running for office, one a man and the other a woman, do you think you would be more inclined to vote for the man or the woman?"

17. Dolan, Kathleen, "Gender Differences in Support for Women Candidates: Is There a Glass Ceiling in American Politics?" *Women and Politics* 17 (1997):27–41; Plutzer, Eric, and John Zipp, "Identity Politics, Partisanship, and Voting for Women Candidates," *Public Opinion Quarterly* 60 (1996):30–57; Rosenthal, Cindy Simon, "The Role of Gender in Descriptive Representation," *Political Research Quarterly* 48 (1995):599–611.

18. Ekstrand, Laurie, and William Eckert, "The Impact of Candidate's Sex on Voter Choice," *Western Political Quarterly* 34 (1981):78–87; Lewis, Carolyn, "Are Women for Women? Feminist and Traditional Values in the Female Electorate," *Women and Politics* 20 (1999):1–28; Sigelman and Welch 1984; Smith, Eric R.A.N., and Richard Fox, "The Electoral Fortunes of Women Candidates for Congress," *Political Research Quarterly* 54 (2001):205–221.

19. Cook 1994; Dolan, Kathleen, "Voting for Women in the 'Year of the Woman,'" *American Journal of Political Science* 42 (1998):272–293.

20. Sigelman and Welch 1984.

21. Thornton, Arland, Duane Alwin, and Donald Camburn, "Causes and Consequences of Sex-Role Attitudes and Attitude Change," *American Sociological Review* 42 (1983):211–227.

22. Races in which two women ran as the major party candidates are excluded from this analysis.

23. Jacobson, Gary, *The Politics of Congressional Elections* (New York: Longman, 2001).

24. The probabilities for ideology, sex, and race are as follows: Ideology—very liberal = .71, very conservative = .41; race—minority = .72, white = .51; sex—woman = .60, man = .50.

25. Krasno, Jonathan, *Challengers, Competition, and Reelection: Comparing House and Senate Elections* (New Haven: Yale University Press, 1994).

26. The probabilities for ideology and age are as follows: Ideology—very liberal = .62, very conservative = .39; age—twenty years old = .41, eighty years old = .60.

27. These are the 1990 and 1996 elections for the House and the 1990, 1996, and 1998 elections for the Senate.

28. Center for the American Woman and Politics (CAWP), *Fact Sheet,* "Women in the U.S. Congress" (New Brunswick, N.J.: Eagleton Institute of Politics, Rutgers University, 2002).

29. Whereas the analysis for 1994 would indicate that Republican women candidates gained some advantage from the national trends at work that year, there was not a significantly larger group of Republican women candidates that year. Indeed, the proportion of Democratic and Republican women candidates is essentially the same from 1992 through 2000. In each of these elections, Democrats made up between 64 and 68 percent of women candidates and Republicans 32 to 36 percent.

30. Most of the studies of actual election results that do find a relationship between voter sex and candidate sex tend to focus exclusively on 1992.

5

Why Vote for
Women Candidates?
The Role of Issues

T HE PREVIOUS CHAPTER provided an opportunity to examine what types of people vote for women candidates. Even though this first step is an important one in understanding public support for women, it is not sufficient. Instead we also want to understand why these people choose women candidates. This second focus requires that we investigate the substance behind a person's vote choice. A lengthy literature on voting has demonstrated time and again that there are a handful of identifiable influences on vote choice. Generally, we know that people base their vote on political party identification, issues, and candidate characteristics. Party identification is considered a relatively stable, long-term influence based on long-standing attitudes about political phenomena. Issue positions and candidate characteristics are thought to be more short-term influences because issues and candidate characteristics are often unique to a particular election. Although issues or candidate characteristics in general may be important across elections, the specific influences are likely to change as the events and personalities change from election to election. Because the impact of party identification was discussed in Chapter 4, this analysis will focus more on the role of issues in voting for women candidates.

The Role of Issues in Vote Choice

Few researchers would question the evidence that party, issues, and candidate characteristics are the three main influences on vote choice. And there is significant evidence gathered over time to establish the general primacy of party identification on the vote. But since the 1960s, there has been considerable debate about how often issues are an important part of the average person's vote calculus. The image of the American voter as one who carefully considers his or her position on the important issues of the day when choosing among candidates is part of our democratic folklore.

115

The "good citizen" is assumed to be informed and educated about the issues and the candidates, casting a vote for the candidate most likely to represent his or her interests on these issues. However, the earliest studies of
American voting behavior raised concern about the validity of this portrait of the typical voter. In their classic study of voting behavior in the
1950s, *The American Voter,* Angus Campbell et al. laid out three conditions
necessary for an issue to influence a person's voting decision.[1] First, a voter
must be aware of an issue and have an opinion on it. Second, the voter
must care enough about the issue to factor it into the voting decision.
Third, an opinion must be accompanied by an understanding of which
party or candidate's position is closest to his or her own. Using this framework, the authors find weak evidence of a link between issues and voting
behavior.

However, fairly soon after this, other researchers began to argue that the
picture painted by *The American Voter* was more pessimistic than was war-
ranted and perhaps was capturing a particularly "issue-free" period in our
political history. With the title of their book, *The Changing American
Voter*, Norman Nie et al. indicate that they find evidence of an evolution in
the way voters think about issues and the way these issues are related to
their vote choice.[2] For example, in their analysis they demonstrate that,
whereas the correlation between issue position and vote choice in 1956
was .18, by 1964 it was .49 and remained high through the early 1970s. At
the same time, they demonstrate a decline in the relationship between
party identification and vote choice, signaling that issues were becoming
more important to vote choice and party identification less so. They also
point to an increase in voters' likelihood of referring to issue positions
when evaluating political candidates from the 1950s to the 1970s.[3] Contemporary analysis also supports the notion that issues are a part of the
decision calculus for some voters. Using the same framework as Campbell
et al., Paul Abramson, John Aldrich, and David Rohde demonstrate that,
since 1980, between 40 and 50 percent of the public can meet the three
criteria necessary for issue voting. They also add a fourth criterion to the
three outlined above: that a person must not only see differences between
candidates on an issue of importance but that they must perceive the differences correctly. For example, in the 2000 presidential election, successful issue voters would have needed to see Al Gore's position on issues as

generally more liberal than the positions taken by George W. Bush. Even with this more stringent requirement, 41 percent of the public could be considered as having met the criteria for issue voting.[4]

Since the 1970s, the debate about issues has not been about whether they matter to vote choice but instead about which issues matter and how, primarily in presidential elections. There is a significant amount of research that suggests an important role for economic issues in determining vote choice, with voters being influenced both by national economic conditions (sociotropic voting) and their own immediate economic interests (pocketbook voting).[5] Other work demonstrates the influence on presidential vote choice in the 1990s of such issues as gays in the military,[6] social issues,[7] and abortion.[8] There is even research that suggests that something as distant from most voters' everyday concerns as foreign policy can influence voting under the right circumstances.[9]

However, in examining the role of issues in vote choice, there is contradictory evidence to suggest that issues are not a major influence on vote choice. For example, Jon Dalager found that the ability of voters to recall issues addressed in their state's U.S. Senate campaigns in 1988 was extremely limited.[10] Among respondents in his research, only 35 percent could correctly cite one of the major issues discussed in their Senate campaign. Another 26 percent recalled an issue but were incorrect in their recollection, and another 39 percent could not name any issues at all. Dalager makes the point that voters can't base their votes on issues if they don't have the correct information. This finding cautions us to remember that, although they are an influence on vote choice, issues are not often a primary one, at least for the vast majority of voters.

As stated above, most of the work on the impact of issues on elections has focused on presidential elections. A role for issues in presidential elections makes sense: They are the elections with the highest visibility, the greatest media coverage, and the largest number of sources from which people can gather information about the candidates and their policy positions. If people can use issues to shape their vote choice, we would expect that presidential elections are the venue in which this would happen. But congressional elections are very different from presidential elections in a number of important ways. Indeed, even all congressional elections are not the same. House races are different from

Senate elections, and congressional elections involving an incumbent and a challenger are very different from open-seat races. So we cannot necessarily assume that issues will influence congressional vote choice in the same manner that they can influence presidential vote choice.

Whereas presidential elections are unique because of their visibility, media saturation, and centrality to our political and governmental system, congressional elections, particularly races for the House of Representatives, are exactly the opposite. Senate elections are somewhat more like presidential elections: They are statewide contests that achieve some measure of visibility on the political landscape, they are usually contested by prominent candidates, and they usually attract considerable media attention. House races, on the other hand, are usually pretty low-key elections that do not command widespread attention from the public or the media. As such, the issue content of these races tends to be low, and a different set of influences shapes vote choice. Indeed, some researchers would suggest that the average congressional voter makes a vote decision based on relatively little information. For example, Paul Herrnson notes that in a House race between an incumbent and a challenger, only about 12 percent of the public can name both candidates. For an open-seat race, about 37 percent can name both candidates. Although larger numbers of people can *recognize* the names of both candidates in House races (as opposed to the more difficult task of recalling them), this finding still indicates the limited amount of information that people possess about congressional elections.[11]

Because of the nature of congressional races—particularly those for the House of Representatives—as low-information elections, the power of incumbency and party identification on vote choice are enhanced. With little candidate or issue information to utilize, voters in congressional elections are most often influenced by their political party or their evaluation of the incumbent (if there is one). The power of these variables may make it difficult for issue considerations to contribute to an individual's voting calculus.

Finally, we must consider the role candidates play in shaping campaign environments in which issues may be a larger or smaller focus. Certainly incumbents, women or men, are less likely to campaign on the basis of issue positions and are more likely to play up their accomplishments and their positive image within the district or state. Challengers, who are often unknown to the public, are the ones who need to distinguish themselves. In the absence of a track record of service, they may well want to focus attention on their issue positions as they attempt to attract voters. But, because many challengers, particularly House challengers, run underfunded campaigns, this battle is often an uphill one. Open-seat races are the ones in which there is the most likely focus on candidate issue positions. Yet, because open-seat races are a small percentage of congressional races every two years, the overall focus on issues in congressional elections is generally low. For all of the reasons cited here, we might expect issues to be a less central element of vote choice in congressional elections.

Issues and Voting for Women

The assumption that issues are relevant to vote choice when women candidates are running for election stems from the literature that examines the stereotypes people hold about women candidates. Stereotyped thinking about women candidates is believed to be important because it can cause people to choose or reject these women based on the public's ideas about their interests and capabilities. As the research cited in Chapter 3 demonstrates, voters often hold clearly gender-based stereotypes about women, assuming that they are best suited to deal with such issues as education, the environment, and children's issues and are less well suited to handle crime, foreign affairs, and economic matters. Stereotyped thinking can be problematic in that it is often not based on reality and can distort the record and accomplishments of both women and men candidates.

Stereotypes can be used by voters to form an overall assessment of a candidate's competence, and if voters consistently stereotype women candidates in a negative fashion, then they may use this assessment as the basis for a negative vote. But stereotypes can also work in conjunction with issue positions to affect vote choice. For example, if a voter holds the stereotyped view that women candidates will not be effective on foreign policy issues and that voter is particularly concerned about foreign policy, then he or she may vote against a woman candidate on this basis. At the same time, of course, stereotypes of women can work in their favor. Women candidates are usually given the edge on such issues as education.

If education is an issue of concern in a particular election, voters may be drawn to support women candidates because of their assumed superiority on this issue.

To determine whether stereotyped thinking about women candidates and issues has any impact on vote choice when a woman candidate is present in congressional elections, I test a model that focuses on some of the major issues on which the public displays significantly stereotyped thinking about the abilities and interests of women candidates, both positively and negatively. These issues are defense, social welfare, public school education, child care, and abortion.[12] If stereotypes about women candidates are relevant to their electoral fortune, I would expect people who want an increase in spending for social welfare, child care, and public schools and voters who are pro-choice to be more likely to vote for women. Additionally, because people tend to think that women are not well suited to handle defense issues, people who want increases in government spending in this area would be less likely to choose the woman candidate. One final variable in the model is not an issue per se but is instead an attitude toward women that is likely to influence a person's general predisposition toward women candidates. This attitude, measured as respondents' feelings toward the women's movement, should move those people who have warmer feelings for the women's movement toward support for a woman congressional candidate. Also included in the model as control variables are the incumbency status of the woman candidate; shared party identification of the respondent and woman candidate; and the party identification, ideology, and sex of the respondent. Coding for all variables in the analysis is found in Appendix B.

As with the analysis of the NES data in Chapter 4, the first step involves the pooled data for the House and Senate elections from 1990 to 2000.[13] Table 5.1 displays the findings for this analysis. The first thing to note, as was apparent in previous analyses, is the significant influence of incumbency and shared political party on vote choice. For elections to both the House and the Senate, party correspondence between the respondent and the woman candidate has the largest impact on the decision to vote for the woman; incumbency is the second most powerful influence. Again, this information indicates that these two factors operate independent of candidate sex; women candidates are advantaged by these influences in the

TABLE 5.1:
Issue Determinants of Support for Women Candidates for Congress
National Election Study 1990–2000 Pooled Analysis
(Logistic Regression Coefficients)

	House of Representatives[1]		Senate	
Woman Incumbent	1.092**	(.49)	.508**	(.25)
Party Identification	.087	(.13)	-.003	(-.00)
Shared Party	2.869**	(.61)	2.563**	(.56)
Ideology	-.076	(-.11)	-.136	(-.20)
Sex	.333#	(.08)	-.079	(.02)
Defense	.210	(.10)	-.194	(-.10)
Social Welfare	.055	(.03)	.140	(.07)
Public Schools	-.004	(-.00)	.336*	(.17)
Child Care	.029	(.01)	.006	(.00)
Abortion	.132	(.10)	.194*	(.14)
Feeling—Women's Movement	.020**	(.46)	.011**	(.26)
Year = 1990	-.723#	(-.18)	-1.337**	(-.30)
Year = 1994	-.594#	(-.15)	-.129	(.03)
Year = 1996	-.190	(-.04)	.325	(.08)
Year = 2000	-.483	(-.12)	.205	(.05)
Constant	-3.439**		-2.167**	
N =	830		1018	
Chi Square =	440.109		433.611	
PRE =	60.41		56.01	

**p < .01; *p < .05; #p < .10

[1]The impact coefficient, in parentheses, gives the change in the probability for the woman candidate as you move from the lowest to the highest value of the independent variables, with all other variables set to their means.

same ways that men are. In terms of demographics, the findings here are very similar to those presented in Chapter 4. The sex of the respondent is also related to voting for a woman in House elections, with women being marginally more likely to vote for the woman candidate than were men. This relationship is not present, however, in Senate elections.

With regard to the impact of issues on vote choice, the data demonstrate important differences between House and Senate elections. For the House, the only other variable significantly related to voting for a woman is the respondent's feeling toward the women's movement: People with warmer feelings are more likely to vote for the woman than those who feel colder toward the movement. For Senate elections, however, issues appear to play a more central role in vote choice. Two issues are significantly associated with choosing the woman—public schools and abortion. Each of these relationships is in the expected direction, by which we mean in a direction consistent with the stereotypes that people hold about the abilities of women candidates. This means that respondents who supported an increase in spending on schools, along with pro-choice voters, are more likely to vote for the woman candidate. Also, as with House elections, stronger feelings for the women's movement are associated with voting for the woman candidate. That demographics (respondent sex) are more important to vote choice in House races, and issues more so in Senate races, is consistent with existing knowledge about the fundamental differences between these two types of elections.[14] House elections are still generally low-visibility elections where issues play a lesser role in vote choice than candidate characteristics and party. Senate elections, however, are much more high visibility affairs, which tends to increase the attention to issues in those elections. Finally, unlike the analysis presented in Chapter 4, the variables accounting for each of the years included in the pooled data set demonstrate only a marginally significant influence on the likelihood of voting for women.

The relative impact of the variables significant to voting for a woman (all other variables set to their mean values) in each type of election is outlined in Figures 5.1 (House) and 5.2 (Senate). As was the case in the analysis of demographic influences on voting for women outlined in Chapter 4, shared political party and incumbency status have the strongest impact on the likelihood of choosing a woman candidate for both the House and the Senate. For House races, feelings toward the women's movement have the next strongest impact. The probability that a respondent with very positive feelings toward the women's movement would chose a woman candidate is .71, whereas for those whose feelings are considerably cooler, the probability is .25. Again, the impact of sex is present but limited. The probability of a woman voter choosing a woman in a race for the House is .58, but for men, the probability is .50. Although

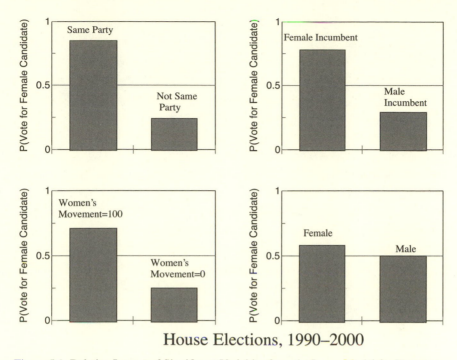

House Elections, 1990–2000

Figure 5.1: Relative Impact of Significant Variables from the Issues Model for House Elections

it is accurate to say that women are more likely than men to support women candidates, the differences are relatively small and require that we acknowledge that voter sex is a significant but secondary influence on support for women candidates.

In the analysis of Senate races, shared party exerts the biggest impact on voting for a woman, followed by the incumbency status of the woman. Among the other influences, positive feelings toward the women's movement have the greatest impact. The probability that someone with very positive feelings toward the women's movement will chose a woman candidate is .60, but it is .32 for those with much cooler attitudes. Abortion and position on public schools also exhibit an impact on voting for a woman. Pro-choice voters and those in favor of increased support for public schools each have about a .53 likelihood of voting for a woman candidate, whereas the probability that pro-life voters or those seeking cuts in education spending will do so is .30.

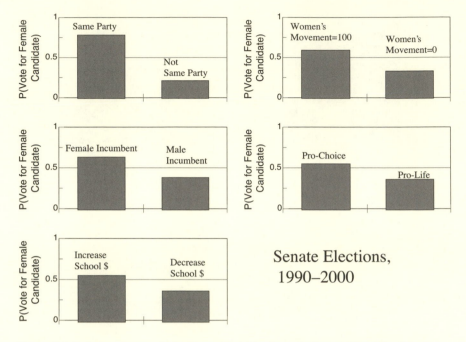

Figure 5.2: Relative Impact of Significant Variables from the Issues Model for Senate Elections

Individual Election Years

Issues are considered a short-term influence on vote choice because the issues important to any particular election are not necessarily the same as the issues important in the election immediately preceding or following it. Because the impact of issues in general, and of individual issues in specific, can vary across elections, it is important to take each election year separately and to examine whether any issues have a consistent influence on voting for a woman during the period under study. Table 5.2 presents the findings for four House elections.[15] Here again we see that, in each election year, shared party identification between the voter and the woman candidate is the most important influence on choosing the woman, followed by the consistent influence of incumbency.

Interestingly, in 1994, respondent party identification is significantly related to voting for a woman, above and beyond a shared party identification.

TABLE 5.2:
Issue Determinants of Support for Women Candidates for U.S. House
(Logistic Regression Coefficients)[1]

	1992	1994	1996	2000
Woman Incumbent	1.350**	.905**	1.430**	1.955**
Party Identification	.154	.304*	.136	-.294#
Party Correspondence	2.426**	3.615**	3.669**	2.482**
Ideology	-.228	-.093	.338#	.074
Sex	.654#	.248	-.185	.372
Defense	.231	.083	-.583*	-.417
Social Welfare	.253	.661#	-.088	-.009
Public Schools	-.076	-.706	-.068	-.071
Child Care	.220	.751	.196	-.328
Abortion	.242	.615*	.215	-.330
Feeling—Women's Movement	.018#	.029*	.043**	.009
Constant	-4.286*	-8.475*	-7.261*	.412
N =	237	164	222	130
Chi Square =	126.089	89.054	138.290	63.106
PRE =	32.894	33.333	49.333	25.000

**p < .01; *p < .05; #p < .10

[1]The data for 1990 are not included because the number of respondents in the model is too small to support analysis. Also, 1998 is excluded because the NES did not ask respondents the same questions that were asked in the other surveys.

Here Republicans are more likely to choose the woman than are Democrats. Although perhaps not what we might usually expect from Republican voters (based on party stereotypes), we must keep in mind that, in 1994, the Republican Party won control of both the House and Senate. This influence of party identification could be driven by Republicans who were responding to a visible group of Republican women candidates for the House.

Beyond the control variables, issues exhibit only a limited influence on vote choice in any given House election. When issues are relevant, they appear to be in line with people's stereotypes about women candidates. For example, in 1994, those who favored higher spending on social welfare programs were more likely to choose women candidates, whereas in 1996, women candidates were favored by those who wanted lower levels of defense spending. Abortion was only significant to vote choice in 1994, with pro-choice women being more likely to vote for women candidates. Positive feelings toward the women's movement demonstrates the most consistent influence, pushing people toward women in 1994 and 1996 but only reaching marginal significance in 1992.

The year-by-year analysis of Senate elections shows the same limited influence of issues in any given election. Party correspondence remains the most important influence on vote choice, with people being overwhelmingly likely to vote for the woman candidate when she is a member of their party. Interestingly, this effect is not evident in 1992, but the standard measure of party identification is, indicating that Democrats in this year were more likely to vote for the woman candidate than were Republicans. This result is a function of the women candidates in that year and the NES data itself. In 1992, ten of the 11 women Senate candidates were Democrats. All ten of these women ran in states represented in the NES sample, whereas the one Republican woman was not. Therefore, Democrats in the sample in 1992 *were* more likely to support the women candidates, who also happened to share their party affiliation.

The woman candidate being the incumbent also continues to influence vote choice in her favor. But note that the coefficients for Senate elections are smaller than for House races. This finding is consistent with our knowledge that the effects of incumbency in Senate elections are a bit weaker than the similar effects in House races.[16] Also, note that incumbency is not a significant influence on voting for women in 2000, the first time that this relationship is observed. All six women who ran for the Senate ran in states that were included in the National Election Study sample.[17] Three were incumbents, and three were challengers. Why none of the incumbents in that year accrued the traditional advantage among voters is unclear.

As with House elections, when issues are significant to voting for a woman, they are in line with people's stereotypes about women's abilities. Pro-choice voters chose women more often than did pro-life voters in 1992 and 2000, but not in 1990 or 1994. Positive feelings toward the women's movement moved people to vote for women in 1992 and 1994, but not in other years. In 1994, those in favor of increased spending on

TABLE 5.3:
Issue Determinants of Support for Women Candidates for U.S. Senate
(Logistic Regression Coefficients)[1]

	1990	1992	1994	2000
Woman Incumbent	1.628*	.653**	.604*	.383
Party Identification	.014	-.534**	-.109	-.048
Party Correspondence	1.525**	-.316	3.159**	3.439**
Ideology	-.060	-.319**	.039	.078
Sex	.540	.020	-.685#	.330
Defense	.022	-.289	-.205	.078
Social Welfare	.554	.281	-.232	.252
Public Schools	.539	.232	.536#	-.151
Child Care	.502	-.011	-.135	-.596#
Abortion	-.042	.371*	.087	.375#
Feeling—Women's Movement	-.010	.020**	.020*	.005
Constant	-3.647	.447	-1.850	-2.928
N =	124	377	223	226
Chi Square =	25.277	186.708	106.376	131.169
PRE =		39.455	55.681	58.536

**p < .01; *p < .05; #p < .10

[1]The data for 1996 are not included because the number of respondents in the model is too small to support analysis. Also, 1998 is excluded because the NES did not ask respondents the same questions that were asked in the other surveys.

public schools were more likely to choose women candidates than those who did not favor increases. Although these year-by-year findings suggest a pattern of inconsistent influence for issues on vote choice, we must remember that the pooled analysis provides the greatest variation across types of candidates and contexts and therefore provides a better picture of the general effect of the issue variables.

Given our general understanding that issues can have an impact on vote choice, but usually a limited one, the results of this analysis should not be terribly surprising. The literature on congressional elections demonstrates that incumbency and party are by far the most significant influences on congressional vote choice. This analysis conforms to that expectation. Further, we know that issues of the nature of those examined here are, themselves, hopelessly intertwined with party affiliation and can generally be expected to play a more limited role in sub-presidential elections, which also is borne out by these findings. Further, because few issues exert the same pull on the public and the candidates over several elections, it may be the case that the issues identified here were not central to the individual elections in which women candidates took part. Finally, the analysis presented here is limited to those issues that were included in the NES. It is possible that other issues have a sex-specific effect but were not available for this analysis.

Ultimately, what this analysis might indicate is that stereotyped thinking about women candidates may not consistently factor into voting decisions in the way previous research had expected. Because much of the past work on stereotypes of women has been carried out using hypothetical elections and experimental situations, our understanding of the link between stereotype and action toward a woman candidate has been limited. As the analysis of evaluations of women candidates in Chapter 3 demonstrated, people sometimes do engage in stereotyped evaluations of women seeking political office. But there is less evidence that they employ those stereotypes when faced with an actual woman candidate. Even though this appears to be true at the congressional level, it may be even more likely the case for lower levels of office where issues may be even less a part of most campaigns for office.

Notes

1. Campbell, Angus, Philip Converse, Warren Miller, and Donald Stokes, *The American Voter* (Ann Arbor: Survey Research Center: University of Michigan, 1960).

2. Nie, Norman, Sidney Verba, and John Petrocik, *The Changing American Voter* (Cambridge, Mass.: Harvard University Press, 1976).

3. Ibid., pp. 165–167.

4. Abramson, Paul, John Aldrich, and David Rohde, *Change and Continuity in the 2000 Elections* (Washington, D.C.: CQ Press, 2002).

5. Clarke, Harold, and Marianne Stewart, "Prospections, Retrospections, and Rationality: The 'Bankers' Model of Presidential Approval Reconsidered," *American Journal of Political Science* 38 (1994):1104–1123; Fiorina, Morris, *Retrospective Voting in American National Elections* (New Haven: Yale University Press, 1981); Kinder, Donald, Gordon Adams,

and Paul Gronke, "Economics and Politics in the 1984 American Presidential Election," *American Journal of Political Science* 33 (1989):491–515.

6. Miller, Warren, and Merrill Shanks, *The New American Voter* (Cambridge, Mass.: Harvard University Press, 1996).

7. Smith, Charles, Peter Radcliffe, and John Kessel, "The Partisan Choice: Bill Clinton or Bob Dole?" in *Reelection 1996: How America Voted*, eds. Herbert Weisberg and Janet Box-Steffensmeier (New York: Chatham House, 1999).

8. Abramowitz, Alan, "It's Abortion, Stupid: Policy Voting in the 1992 Presidential Election," *Journal of Politics* 57 (1995):176–186; Alvarez, R. Michael, and Jonathan Nagler, "Economics, Entitlements, and Social Issues: Voter Choice in the 1996 Presidential Election," *American Journal of Political Science* 42 (1998):1349–1363.

9. Aldrich, John, John Sullivan, and Eugene Borgida, "Foreign Affairs and Issue Voting: Do Presidential Candidates 'Waltz Before a Blind Audience'?" *American Political Science Review* 83 (1989):123–141.

10. Dalager, Jon, "Voters, Issues, and Elections: Are the Candidates' Messages Getting Through?" *Journal of Politics* 58 (1996):486–515.

11. Herrnson, Paul, *Congressional Elections: Campaigning at Home and in Washington,* 3rd ed. (Washington, D.C.: CQ Press, 2000).

12. For each of the spending issues, the NES asks respondents whether they think that federal government spending on each issue area should be increased, decreased, or kept about the same.

13. Data for 1998 are excluded from this analysis. The NES survey in 1998 was very short, which resulted in very few issue questions being asked of respondents.

14. Jacobson, Gary, *The Politics of Congressional Elections,* 5th ed. (New York: Longman, 2001).

15. The analysis for 1990 is not included because the number of respondents in the model is too small to support accurate conclusions.

16. Jacobson 2001.

17. The six were Dianne Feinstein (CA), Olympia Snowe (ME), Debbie Stabenow (MI), Hillary Rodham Clinton (NY), Kay Bailey Hutchison (TX), and Maria Cantwell (WA). Jean Carnahan (MO), who informally took her husband's place on the ballot for U.S. Senate after his death three weeks before the 2000 election, was not included in this analysis.

6

The Role of the
Electoral Environment

IN CHAPTERS 4 AND 5 we saw that an examination of who votes for women candidates for Congress revealed a limited role for the influence of individual demographic characteristics and issue positions on vote choice. In some circumstances, women, minorities, older people, and the less religious were more likely to choose a woman candidate for the House or Senate than other voters. With regard to issues, defense, child care, women's rights, and attitudes toward the women's movement were periodically significant to voting for a woman. But one interesting aspect of this analysis is the disparity between some of the findings of the pooled analysis and those of the individual election years. The pooled analysis offers a general picture of the patterns of support for women candidates during the ten-year period. The inconsistencies between the two are revealed in the either weak or nonsignificant findings in various election years, which may be a function of the smaller sample sizes in the individual years. What this suggests is that individual characteristics, attitudes, and issue positions can play a role in shaping vote choice when a woman candidate is present but that these factors are not, in and of themselves, significant, ongoing influences.

Why might this be the case? Why might women have been more likely to vote for women candidates than were men in 1992 but not before or since? Why would people who supported decreases in defense spending be more likely to vote for women only in 1996? Why would these voters behave in ways that are consistent with expectations from the stereotyping literature, but only in certain election years? I would suggest that there is another important consideration at work, that of the environment or context of a particular election. Perhaps some electoral environments are more conducive to allowing people to identify that their personal or issue interests may be best represented by a woman candidate. Perhaps the ability of women candidates to mobilize voters who might naturally support them is shaped by the electoral environment.

Certainly, the role of candidate sex and its impact on voters is a complex relationship. Recent work on the "gender basis of electoral behavior" suggests that "gender matters differently and to different degrees in different elections" because of a complex interaction of voter, candidate, party, and environmental influences.[1] Virginia Sapiro and Pamela Johnston Conover use the "Year of the Woman" election of 1992 as a case study of the complex nature of candidate sex and gender issues in elections: Women candidates for Congress were prominent, but their success was influenced by structural as well as political considerations; the gender gap was variable across several Senate races and the presidential election; and gender issues played differently in certain states and certain races. They suggest that these findings provide evidence of the fact that gender does not operate in one consistent fashion as an electoral influence and that "context is a crucial mediator in creating gender differences in voting."[2]

Considering the context of a particular election or series of elections is an important element in understanding the gender dynamic in elections. We must recognize that each election environment is shaped by unique candidate, party, and political influences and that these factors can have an impact on whether candidate sex and gender-related issues will have a significant role in shaping voter behavior. It may be misleading to suggest, then, that certain voters will be more likely to support women candidates because of their personal characteristics or issue positions in every, or even most, elections. Instead, it may be that aspects of the election or its environment stimulate voters to focus on those interests and thereby make a connection to a particular candidate. For example, work on the impact of campaigns suggests that the "major effect of political campaigns may be to activate people's existing predispositions or 'enlighten' the preferences of voters so as to bring their votes into alignment with their social and economic interests."[3] Here the argument is that variables such as sex, race, or religion only "become relevant if some political force makes them relevant, as when candidates or parties raise relevant issues."[4]

This chapter explores whether the "electoral environment" structures the determinants of vote choice in elections with a woman candidate. The aspect of the environment believed to be important is the amount of gendered information that is available to voters. If voters are to be able to identify that women candidates may best represent their interests, they need information about the candidates and the election issues that would help them make that link. Attention to women candidates, their sex, and the issues on which they campaign would create a particular election environment.

Take, for example, the congressional elections of 1992. Heralded as the "Year of the Woman," the environment of the 1992 election was one with a heavy focus on gender issues: A record number of women ran for Congress that year, and these women candidates received a large amount of attention, as did the so-called "women's issues," such as abortion, family leave, and sexual harassment. Many of the women candidates for Congress ran "as women," focusing on women's underrepresentation in Congress and on their status as outsiders to a scandal-plagued institution. Domestic issues, often seen by voters as a particular strength of women candidates, were especially important that year.[5] Perhaps the most indelible image from this election was the dramatic increase in women elected to Congress, from 31 before the 1992 election to 53 after.[6] Several factors—candidates, issues, structural conditions, electoral context—joined to make 1992 an election year in which gender and gender considerations played an important role.

An argument for the influence of the electoral environment would suggest that the presence of these women candidates and the focus on them and the gender issues they articulated created a unique dynamic that had an impact on voters. Such an argument draws upon research on opinion formation that treats opinion formation as a function of the information to which people are exposed.[7] Here it is suggested that candidate sex and other gender-related issues are pieces of information in the electoral environment being communicated to voters. In a gender-rich environment, the salience and accessibility of these issues is increased, and the likelihood that voters will use them in making a voting decision is increased as well. In such a circumstance, voters rely on gender-related considerations precisely because of the amount of gender-based information available to them. Conversely, voters can't make use of gendered information when it is not as abundant. One possible consequence of an absence of gendered information in elections is that the influence of demographic or issue variables expected to be important in contests involving a woman candidate may not be activated without the stimulation offered by the electoral setting.

There is ample evidence from the election of 1992 that the environment mattered, that the focus on women candidates and gender-related issues had an impact on voters and the public at large. Research demonstrates that the presence of women candidates for Congress or governor significantly increased political discussion among the public, especially among women, and increased the psychological engagement, media attentiveness, and participation of women in the election.[8] Voting behavior was influenced by women candidates and gender issues that year as well. An examination of voting support for women candidates for Congress demonstrated that people who voted for women candidates were different in their personal characteristics and issue concerns than those who voted for men or for Democrats.[9] Also gender gaps, the difference between the voting patterns of women and men, were larger in elections in which the media focused heavily on gender issues, such as in the two California U.S. Senate races involving Barbara Boxer and Dianne Feinstein. According to one researcher, this disparity is because, at least in part, "the context of the election activates basic gender beliefs and identities."[10]

Also supporting the argument that the amount of gendered information in an election environment has an impact on voter attitudes and behaviors is what happens in the absence of that information. None of the elections before or since 1992 has had as significant a focus on candidate sex and gender issues, and media attention to women candidates has waned somewhat.[11] Not coincidentally, research on other election years indicates that none of the dynamics described above involving the impact of women candidates was present in elections before or after 1992.[12]

Nor is the impact of women candidates one of number. The number of women running for Congress in 1992 was a record to that point. But each election cycle since has seen an increase in the number of women candidates, with no corresponding attitudinal or behavioral impact on voters to that documented in 1992. It is not just the presence of a woman candidate that can alter the electoral environment, but instead it is a complex dynamic that includes the presence of women candidates and enough media attention to them and gendered issues to allow voters to become aware of these women and have their predispositions to vote for them activated. As this suggests, if the gendered electoral environment is going to have an impact, voters must be able to consume the gendered information and act upon it. Research on the impact of information on people's attitudes and beliefs indicates that people are not equal in their ability to receive and to act on information in the electoral environment.[13] This ability depends on a person's level of political awareness. Philip Converse argues that people with high levels of awareness may be best able to receive information from the political environment, but they may also have the most well-developed ideas about politics and could resist new information more easily. Those with low levels of awareness may pay too little attention to politics to be exposed to, or to absorb, new information. People in the middle, however, may be aware enough to receive information and open enough to be influenced by it.[14] This means that another important consideration is determining to which voters, if any, the amount of gendered information in the electoral environment is relevant. Does the content of the environment relate to voting for a woman for all voters, or does it perhaps related to a subset only? To pinpoint this answer, we need to consider the amount of awareness of politics that respondents exhibit as a gauge of their ability to respond to the environment.

Gendered Information in the Electoral Environment

Although some voters may have contact with a woman candidate during a campaign, the greatest likelihood is that the average voter will encounter a woman candidate or gendered election and issue information through the media. To measure the content of media attention to women candidates, I conducted an analysis of the number of newspaper stories about women candidates that appeared in local and national newspapers from September 1 to the day before the election for each year from 1990 to 2000, with the exception of 1998.[15] The "U.S. News" section of Lexis-Nexis was employed, using the search phrases "women candidates" and "election." Figure 6.1 displays the trend in the number of articles on women candidates appearing during each general election period. As the data suggest, 1992 was a year unique in the amount of attention given to women candidates. This attention, as measured by newspaper articles, is an enormous leap over the press coverage women candidates received immediately prior to this in 1990 and falls sharply in 1994, continuing a dramatic decline through the election of 2000.

It is important to note that this coverage of women candidates bears no relationship to the number of women running in each year. Indeed, as the second part of Figure 6.1 demonstrates, the number of women candidates running for Congress has increased steadily since 1990. If media attention to women candidates was a function of the number running, we would expect the trend displayed in the first part of Figure 6.1 to mirror that of the second part: More women running should mean more coverage of women candidates. But instead, as Sue Carroll observed, "The Year of the Woman frame (in 1992) proved to be a mixed blessing. One of the major downsides was that women candidates seemed to be old news after 1992 and the media paid very little attention to women candidates in 1994 or 1996."[16] This pattern she observed clearly continued through 2000.

Does Gendered Information in the Environment Matter?

As a first step in testing whether the amount of gendered information in the electoral environment has any impact on voting for women candidates, data on the context of the electoral environment were merged with the data from the 1990–1996 and 2000 NES files to create a pooled data set that covers the period under consideration. Table 6.1 offers a simple model of the determinants of voting for a woman candidate based on the four traditional major influences on vote choice: incumbency status of the woman, party identification of the respondent, ideology of the respondent, and a shared party identification between the respondent and the woman candidate. To this I add a variable measuring the amount of gendered information in the electoral environment based on the media analysis outlined earlier in the chapter. This analysis examines whether the amount of gendered information has an impact on voting for a woman candidate after we consider the impact of incumbency, party, and ideology.

To determine whether information is more important to some voters than others, the analysis is conducted for the sample as a whole and then

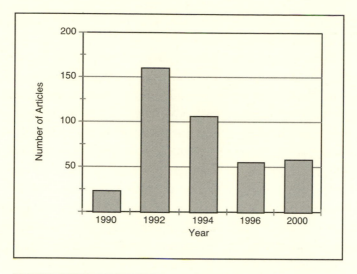

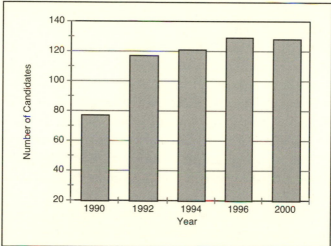

Figure 6.1: Number of Newspaper Articles About Women Candidates and Number of Women Candidates 1990–2000

for subgroups of people based on their level of political awareness. Respondents are categorized as having low/moderate or high levels of awareness.[17] According to John Zaller, the amount of gendered information should be most relevant to the voting decisions of those with more moderate levels of political awareness. Table 6.1 presents the data for both the House and the Senate. In elections for the House, the amount of gendered information available to the public is significantly related to support for women candidates, even when controlling for the more traditional influences on vote choice. When there is more gendered information in the environment, people are more likely to vote for women. In looking at respondents based on their level of political awareness, the data demonstrate that the influence of information is significant for people with low/moderate levels of awareness but not for those whose awareness is higher. As the impact coefficient demonstrates, respondents with lower political awareness are 23 percent more likely to vote for a woman House candidate in a more gender-rich election environment. This finding is consistent with the idea that the amount of gendered information may well serve to help people make the connection between their own interests and the presence of women candidates. Absent that information, people may not make the connection and may be less likely to choose a woman.

That this variable is significant in House races makes sense, as elections for the House are traditionally considered low-information elections that don't receive a large amount of media attention. Further, the significant impact of context on those with low levels of awareness also makes sense: These people don't have a vast store of information to draw upon when approaching politics. Therefore, information available in the environment can become an important source for them. People with higher levels of awareness start out with more information and may not have to rely on the electoral environment to provide it for them.

Senate races exhibit a different pattern. Here the amount of gendered information in the electoral environment is not significantly related to voting for women, either for the sample as a whole or among respondents based on their levels of information. Senate elections, as opposed to House races, are statewide affairs that usually receive extensive media coverage. Because of this, information about Senate candidates is probably more readily available to all voters, regardless of awareness, because the information will be much more easily accessed. The naturally occurring focus on issues in Senate elections may make heightened attention to gender issues unnecessary for voters to make the connection between themselves and a woman candidate.

TABLE 6.1:
Determinants of Support for Women Candidates
Party, Incumbency, and Electoral Environment
National Election Study Data 1990–2000

House of Representatives

	All Respondents[1]	Low Awareness	High Awareness
Woman Incumbent	.991** (.46)	1.00** (.45)	.983** (.45)
Party Identification	.010 (.02)	.042 (.06)	-.002 (-.01)
Party Correspondence	2.735** (.59)	2.624** (.56)	2.837** (.60)
Ideology	-.222** (-.32)	-.197# (-28)	-.231* (-.33)
Gender Context	.006* (.19)	.006* (.23)	.005 (.15)
Year=1994	-.512* (-.13)	-.700* (-.17)	-.467 (-.11)
Constant	-.590	-.576	-.554
N =	946	377	558
Chi Square =	472.607	175.849	293.24
PRE =	57.10	54.31	61.90

Senate

	All Respondents	Low Awareness	High Awareness
Woman Incumbent	.501** (.25)	.557** (.27)	.488** (.23)
Party Identification	-.027 (-.04)	-.029 (-.04)	-.074 (-.11)
Party Correspondence	2.560** (.56)	2.148** (.48)	2.829* (.61)
Ideology	-.149* (-.22)	-.148 (-21)	-.117 (-.17)
Gender Context	.002 (.08)	.001 (.02)	.004 (.14)
Year = 1990	-1.451** (-.13)	-1.349* (-.21)	-1.433** (-.33)
Year = 1994	-.518* (-.32)	-.899** (-.28)	-.298 (-.07)
Constant	-.424	-.171	-.632
N =	1137	467	667
Chi Square =	464.780	152.420	317.87
PRE =	57.90	47.80	53.703

**p < .01; *p < .05; #p < .10

[1]The impact coefficient, in parentheses, gives the change in the probability of voting for the woman candidate as you move from the lowest to the highest value of each independent variable, with all other variables set to their means.

Demographics, Issues, and Context

To examine further the potential impact of gendered information, two additional models were constructed to test for the impact of the electoral environment on people's likelihood of voting for a woman. The first of these models reflects the demographic characteristics of voters outlined in Chapter 4, whereas the other focuses on the issues addressed in Chapter 5. Each model includes the relevant control variables, demographic or issue variables, a variable that measures the amount of gendered information in the electoral environment, and a series of interaction variables. These interactions combine the demographic or issue variables with the measure of the electoral environment. If the amount of gendered information available influences the relationship between the independent variables and vote choice, then these interaction terms should be significantly related to voting for women.

The analysis is again presented for three groups: the full sample and those with higher and low/moderate levels of political awareness. Because the focus in this discussion is on whether the electoral context is significant to voting for a woman, Tables 6.2 and 6.3 will only present coefficients for demographic, issue, or context variables that reach statistical significance. Table 6.2 presents the findings for the analysis based on the demographic model. Because previous literature, and the analysis presented in Chapter 4, demonstrates the presence of an "affinity effect," the primary demographic variable of interest here is respondent sex.

Taking House races first, the first column in Table 6.2 presents the findings for the sample as a whole, from which it is evident that neither the variable measuring the electoral environment nor the interaction between respondent sex and the environment are related to voting for a woman. Although the findings are not shown, the previously established importance of women's incumbency and shared party affiliation are the primary explanatory variables in voting for a woman. The same situation is true for respondents with high levels of political awareness (column 3), with neither variable being important to their vote choice. But the situation is different, as we may expect, for those with low/moderate awareness. Here the variable measuring the interaction of respondent sex and election context is significantly related to vote choice. Women with lower levels of awareness

TABLE 6.2:
Importance of Electoral Environment to Support for Women Candidates
Demographic Model 1990–2000

House of Representatives

	All Respondents	Low Awareness	High Awareness
Sex	-.037	-.931	.470
Gender Context	.001	-.017	.009
Sex* Gender Context	.005	.014*	-.001
N =	909	366	532
Chi Square =	463.124	179.155	287.808
PRE =	48.870	40.151	52.582

Senate

	All Respondents	Low Awareness	High Awareness
Sex	.018	.569	-.390
Gender Context	.002	.010	-.004
Sex* Gender Context	-.001	-.006	.004
N =	1083	446	634
Chi Square =	456.331	150.587	315.194
PRE =	45.552	25.714	55.246

$**p < .01$; $*p < .05$; $\#p < .10$

are more likely to vote for women candidates when the electoral environment offers more gendered information and are less likely to do so in the absence of such information. This finding supports Converse's contention that information can have the greatest impact among those who are most likely to be able to be affected by it and upholds the idea that the electoral environment is key in helping to determine whether or not people will be able to connect their interests with women and vote accordingly.

For Senate races, the variables measuring the impact of electoral environment and its relationship to respondent sex are not significantly related to voting for women for any respondents, regardless of their political awareness. Given what we know about Senate races as high-visibility elections, it may be that the context of the electoral environment matters less to voters. People with high levels of awareness are unlikely to need the information provided by the election context, but even those with low/moderate awareness may be able to take the information they need from the relatively information-rich atmosphere of a Senate election. But Senate races, in and of themselves, may provide enough information that the presence of a woman candidate or a gendered atmosphere provide limited additional information benefits.

Table 6.3 presents the analysis of the model accounting for the impact of issues and the electoral environment on voting for a woman. In this analysis, the same issue model presented in Chapter 5 is employed. The issues included are defense, social welfare, education, child care, abortion, and attitudes toward the women's movement, both on their own and in interaction with the variable measuring the gendered context of the election. For ease of presentation, only those issue variables that demonstrate a significant relationship to voting for a woman are included in Table 6.3. For House elections, the first column describes the situation for the whole sample. There are four variables that are significantly related to voting for women by themselves: sex of the respondent, defense, abortion, and feelings toward the women's movement. Women, those who support decreases in defense spending, those people who are pro-choice, and those with stronger feelings toward the women's movement are more likely to choose a woman candidate. With regard to the interaction variables in this model, only the interaction between abortion and electoral context is significant in the full sample. This indicates that the significant relationship between abortion and voting for a woman becomes stronger as the amount of gendered information in the environment increases, supporting the argument that the information provided by the electoral environment can change the voting dynamic.

In examining the impact of the information environment on those with lower and higher amounts of political awareness, the argument in favor of the importance of information receives additional support. For example, among those with low/moderate awareness, the sex of the respondent is not related to voting for a woman. But, as the electoral environment becomes more gendered, women become significantly more likely than men to vote for women candidates. The presence of greater amounts of information may work to activate "affinity" voting among women. Again, those

TABLE 6.3:
Importance of Electoral Environment to Support for Women Candidates
Issues Model 1990–2000

House of Representatives

	All Respondents	Low Awareness	High Awareness
Sex	.348*	.422	.255
Sex* Gender Context	.005	.015*	-.002
Defense	-.176*	.326	.148
Defense* Context	-.001	-.012*	.008*
Abortion	.128#	.058	.240
Abortion* Context	.003#	.003	.005*
Feeling—Women's Movement	.019#	.023*	.014*
Women s Movement* Context	.001	.001	.001
N =	830	316	503
Chi Square =	446.246	169.701	297.198
PRE =	49.386	44.827	57.487

Senate

	All Respondents	Low Awareness	High Awareness
Abortion	.193*	.033	.309*
Abortion* Context	.001	.005*	-.001
Feeling—Women's Movement	.011*	.017*	.010*
Women's Movement* Context	.003*	.004*	.003*
N =	1019	408	608
Chi Square =	453.331	160.479	320.645
PRE =	45.600	32.575	50.000

**p < .01; *p < .05; #p < .10

with low awareness are the most in need of information about candidates. Not surprisingly, the interaction between sex and the electoral context is not significant among those with higher levels of political awareness. These people are not in need of information in the same way the other group is and, therefore, are less likely to be affected by the environment.

Abortion also demonstrates a relationship to the electoral environment. For high-awareness respondents, abortion by itself is a significant determinant of voting for women, with pro-choice voters being more likely to vote for women. But the impact of abortion on vote choice becomes even stronger as the electoral environment becomes more heavily gendered. Because abortion is an issue so heavily identified with women candidates, it makes sense that a gendered environment would work to strengthen the impact of a pro-choice position on voting for women. However, the same relationship does not exist among low/moderate-awareness respondents, which runs somewhat counter to expectations.

On the issue of defense, the low and high awareness respondents part ways. First, the issue of defense on its own is not significantly related to voting for a woman candidate for either group. But the interaction of defense and the electoral context is significant for both—in different directions. For those with higher levels of awareness, the amount of gendered information in the environment increases the strength of the relationship between position on defense and choosing a woman candidate. For those respondents with low/moderate awareness, the value of defense as an issue actually weakens as the electoral context becomes more gendered. Those with higher awareness on this issue are better able to use increased gendered information to shape their vote choice, but those with lower awareness are not, which may be because defense is a "male" issue and could represent a more difficult task for low-information voters.

For Senate races, the impact of issues and the electoral context are more limited. In the sample as a whole, abortion and attitudes toward the women's movement are related to voting for a woman by themselves, with pro-choice voters and those with warmer attitudes toward the women's movement being more likely to choose a woman candidate. Although the election context has no relationship to how abortion influences voting, the impact of attitudes toward the women's movement is strengthened by an increase in the amount of gendered information in the environment.

In looking at the impact of abortion across "awareness" groups, the result is consistent with the argument about the importance of the information in the electoral context. For those with low/moderate levels of awareness, abortion by itself is not significantly related to voting for women. However, the interaction between abortion and the electoral environment is significant, indicating that abortion becomes a more important influence on vote choice as the amount of information increases. Among those with higher levels of awareness, abortion on its own is a significant determinant of voting for a woman, but the interaction between abortion and context is not. The finding on abortion is a clear illustration of the argument regarding the importance of information and how it can influence people differently, depending on their level of need for that information.

The only other variable in the Senate issues model that is significant is attitude toward the women's movement. This variable is significant on its own for both those with low/moderate and high levels of awareness. And the interaction of attitudes and electoral environment is also significant for both groups, indicating that the impact of these attitudes becomes even stronger when there is more gendered information available.

In all, there is some evidence to support the argument that aspects of the electoral environment are important to the decision to vote for a woman. The amount of gendered information is important, with more information about candidate sex and gender issues in the election context having a direct impact on vote choice. There is also evidence that the impact of some issues is heightened in such an environment. Both of these findings point to the importance of a focus on candidate sex and gender issues to shaping voting decisions. It also helps explain why the demographic or issue variables examined in Chapters 4 and 5 exhibited an inconsistent influence on vote choice across elections. At some level, the influence of demographic or issue variables may be activated by certain electoral environments, environments in which there is significant attention to candidate sex and gendered issues. The presence of this information increases the accessibility of candidate sex and gendered issues.

The analysis in this chapter also supports the idea that the impact of the information environment is not consistent across people. Those with higher levels of political awareness were less likely to be affected by the amount of gendered information in the environment. As Converse suggests, this finding is explained by the fact that these people are the most likely to receive information from the election regardless of the level of information. But for people with more modest levels of awareness, the amount of information is relevant. Six of the ten relevant coefficients (context in Table 6.1 and interaction terms in Tables 6.2 and 6.3) were significantly related to vote choice for the low/moderate-awareness group, but only three out of ten were significant for the high-awareness group. These are people who may not actively seek out information about candidates in an election, but if the election environment has a particular focus, they can perceive this and take the information into account.

Finally, it is clear that a certain type of influence is activated by the gendered election environment, which can increase its impact on a voter's choice at the ballot box. With the exception of defense, the variables that were significant in this analysis of issues and the election context are those some researchers describe as having manifest gender content.[18] Abortion, feelings toward the women's movement, and respondent sex are all influences on vote choice that have a clear connection to gender issues. Other issues, such as education or the environment, are referred to as latent gender issues: We tend to associate them more closely with women candidates and officeholders than men, but the content of the issues themselves is not directly gendered in nature. Our closer association of education with women candidates is not because education is an issue that necessarily affects women differently than it does men but instead because our stereotypes about women lead us to conclude that they will be more interested in, and capable with, that issue. It may be the case that the gendered focus in a particular election serves to activate or to heighten the influence of those issues that have an obvious and strong link to gender considerations (manifest issues like abortion or child care), but may be less able to strengthen the impact of more latent gender issues, such as education or the environment.

Conclusion

The investigation of the determinants of support for women candidates presented in earlier chapters suggested that there is not one set of voter characteristics or issue positions that is regularly related to voting for a woman. Instead, analysis of congressional elections from 1990 to 2000 indicates that some demographic and issue variables are significant at some times but not others. These findings point to the notion that candidate sex and gender issues are not simple, straightforward political variables that affect all voters in a particular way. Instead, the impact of candidate sex is a complex one that is dependent on the candidate, her party, the voters, and the environment. As a way of explaining these patterns, this chapter advances the argument that electoral context is an important part of the relationship between women candidates and the public. A focus on gender and gender-related issues in an election appears to make it easier for some voters to identify correspondence between their interests and issue positions and women candidates. Understanding the impact that the information environment can have on the fortunes of women candidates helps us draw a more complete picture of recent congressional elections and can bring a bit of order to what can appear to be a haphazard set of influences on voting for women.

Notes

1. Sapiro, Virginia, and Pamela Johnston Conover, "The Variable Gender Basis of Electoral Politics: Gender and Context in the 1992 US Election," *British Journal of Political Science* 27 (1997):523.

2. Ibid., p. 501.

3. Niemi, Richard, and Herbert Weisberg, eds., *Controversies in Voting Behavior,* 4th ed. (Washington, D.C.: CQ Press, 2001), p. 187. See also Gelman, Andrew, and Gary King, "Why Are American Election Polls So Variable When Votes are So Predictable?" *British Journal of Political Science* 23 (1993):409–451.

4. Niemi and Weisberg 2001, p. 188.

5. Burrell, Barbara, *A Woman's Place Is in the House: Campaigning for Congress in the Feminist Era* (Ann Arbor: University of Michigan Press, 1994); Wilcox, Clyde, "Why Was 1992 the 'Year of the Woman'? Explaining Women's Gains in 1992," in *The Year of the Woman: Myths and Realities*, eds. Elizabeth Adell Cook, Sue Thomas, and Clyde Wilcox (Boulder: Westview Press, 1994).

6. Center for the American Woman and Politics (CAWP), *Fact Sheet*, "Women in the U.S. Congress" (New Brunswick, N.J.: Eagleton Institute of Politics, Rutgers University, 2000).

7. Lazarfeld, Paul, Bernard Berelson, and Hazel Gaudet, *The People's Choice: How the Voter Makes up His Mind in a Presidential Campaign*, 3rd ed. (New York: Columbia University Press, 1968); Zaller, John, *The Nature and Origins of Mass Opinion* (New York: Cambridge University Press, 1992).

8. Hansen, Susan, "Talking About Politics: Gender and Contextual Effects on Political Proselytizing," *Journal of Politics* 59 (1997):73–103; Koch, Jeffrey, "Candidate Gender and

Women's Psychological Engagement in Politics," *American Politics Quarterly* 25 (1997): 118–133; Sapiro and Conover 1997.

9. Dolan, Kathleen, "Voting for Women in the 'Year of the Woman,'" *American Journal of Political Science* 42 (1998):272–293.

10. Cook, Elizabeth, "Voter Reaction to Women Candidates," in *Women and Elective Office: Past, Present, and Future*, eds. Sue Thomas and Clyde Wilcox (New York: Oxford University Press, 1998).

11. Carroll, Susan, "The Disempowerment of the Gender Gap: Soccer Moms and the 1996 Elections," *PS: Political Science and Politics* 32 (1999):7–12; Foerstel, Karen, "For Women Candidates, an Uncertain Season," *CQ Weekly* 56 (1998):39; Fox, Richard, *Gender Dynamics in Congressional Elections* (Thousand Oaks, Calif.: Sage Publications, 1997); Harwood, John, and Gerald Seib, "Female Democrats Lack Issues That Led to '92 Success," *Wall Street Journal*, Eastern ed., December 9, 1997; Rubin, Alissa, "1994 Elections Are Looking Like the 'Off-Year' of the Woman," *CQ Weekly*, October 15, 1994.

12. Dolan, Kathleen, "Electoral Context, Issues, and Voting for Women in the 1990s," *Women and Politics* 23 (2001):21–36; Hansen 1997; Koch 1997.

13. Converse, Philip, "Information Flow and the Stability of Partisan Attitudes," *Public Opinion Quarterly* 26 (1962):578–599; Zaller, John, "The Diffusion of Political Attitudes," *Journal of Personality and Social Psychology* 58 (1987): 821–837.

14. Converse 1962; Zaller 1992.

15. The National Election Study survey instrument for 1998 was very limited and did not ask most of the candidate and issue questions that are asked in all other years. For this reason, comparable questions do not exist. Therefore, 1998 is excluded from this analysis.

16. Carroll 1999, p. 9.

17. Categorizing people as having low/moderate and high levels of political awareness is done using the variable that records the NES interviewer's perception of the amount of information about politics that each respondent possessed. Using more standard measures of political awareness is not possible when analyzing both presidential and midterm elections because the NES does not ask comparable questions across all years. Also, although Converse and Zaller advocate creating three categories of awareness (low, medium, and high), this is not possible when the dependent variable is a variable that measures voting behavior. Those who would be categorized as having low levels of awareness are the least likely to have voted or to have answered the political ideology question, which means that they are mostly eliminated from the analysis of voting for women candidates. Therefore, low and moderately aware people are put together, and high-awareness people are in their own category.

18. Iyengar, Shanto, Nicholas Valentino, Stephen Ansolabehere, and Adam Simon, "Running as a Woman: Gender Stereotyping in Women's Campaigns," in *Women, Media, and Politics* (New York: Oxford University Press, 1997).

7

....

Conclusions:
The Role of Candidate
Sex in American Elections

THROUGHOUT THE COURSE of our nation's history, the prospect of a woman running for elected office has gone from being a scandalous, inconceivable event to one that is widely supported and increasingly common. The women who run for office in the contemporary period face a political and social world that is much more welcoming. Yet we still, in journalistic, popular, and academic accounts of their activities, refer to them as "women candidates." That we modify the noun "candidates" in this way indicates that candidate sex still a relevant, or at least obvious, aspect of their electoral activities.

Key to understanding the changing fortunes of women candidates is understanding their relationship with the public. Certainly, as history indicates, women candidates have been affected by structural and institutional barriers, such as electoral rules and political parties. But the reactions of potential voters to these women are perhaps most important to taking a measure of their status in politics. Public evaluation of women's place in politics in general, and in elected office in specific, has gone from overtly hostile to largely supportive. Although some resistance may remain, few people in the United States today see women as unsuited for political activity.

Whether and how this acceptance translates into voting support is less clearly understood. The paucity of women candidates for much of our history hampered attempts by researchers to examine the dynamics involved in people's decision to vote for or against a woman candidate. A large literature based on aggregate and experimental analysis provided a rich basis for understanding how and when candidate sex is relevant to people's evaluations of candidates. More recently, as the number of women running has increased, the number of people facing the choice of voting for a woman has increased as well. This occasion has given researchers fresh opportunities to determine how candidate sex operates in the "real world" of elections.

Major Findings

One of the major conclusions of the analysis of voter response to women candidates conducted here is that candidate sex, and the gendered considerations it can raise, has a more complex and nuanced impact on voters than we may have imagined. In looking at how voters evaluated and chose (or failed to choose) women candidates for Congress during a ten-year period, the primary conclusion that can be drawn is that the presence of women candidates, in most cases, does not influence the public in one particular direction. The ways in which respondents in this analysis evaluated women and the patterns of who voted for them and why were not consistent over the six elections examined. In some elections, women voters were more likely to support women candidates, but not in others. In some years, such issues as abortion or defense were related to choosing women candidates, but not always. That there is no constant pattern to the way people behave in the presence of women candidates tells us that the impact of their sex is, in part, conditioned by external forces.

Another significant conclusion drawn from this project is the importance of political party to a consideration of voter reaction to women candidates. Several authors have outlined how the public can respond differently to women candidates based on their political party.[1] This is one way in which the literature based on hypotheticals and experiments is most severely limited. By focusing exclusively on candidate sex, these works create an artificial situation that, although successful at isolating reactions to candidate sex, fails to replicate the more complicated evaluations people must make in the real political world. Political party remains the primary way by which the public evaluates the political world, and it should not surprise us that they continue to do so in the presence of women candidates. Time and again the results of this project point to the important influence of political party.

Candidate Evaluations

With regard to the ways that people evaluate women candidates, it is clear that people assess Democratic and Republican women differently. In the pooled analysis of the six congressional elections from 1990 to 2000 presented in Chapter 3, candidate sex was significantly related to people's evaluations of the ideology of Democratic candidates, but it was not related to evaluations of Republicans. Respondents perceived Democratic women to be more liberal than Democratic men, but they saw no difference between women and men Republicans. Party was also important to conditioning evaluations based on issue stereotypes. Respondents were significantly more likely to evaluate Democratic candidates in terms of traditional female issues when that Democrat was a woman. There were no differences in the issues people employed to evaluate Republican women and men. The only evaluation for which party was not relevant was salience. Here, people were more likely to have more information about women candidates, both Democratic and Republican, than about men of either party.

The importance of political party to people's evaluations of women candidates is probably related to an interaction between the partisan stereotypes and gender-based stereotypes that people employ when considering political information. As discussed earlier, there is a fair degree of correspondence between the partisan stereotypes that people hold about Democrats and those they hold about women. Both Democrats and women are perceived to be more concerned with social issues, issues of working class people, and women's issues. The reverse is true as well, that stereotypes of Republicans and men appear to overlap. What this stereotyping may mean for women candidates is that Democratic women present an "easier" evaluation task for people because of the consistency of the two major stereotypes they trigger. Republican women, on the other hand, are more difficult for people to assess because stereotypes about their party and their sex are in conflict.

As the year-by-year analysis suggests, the stereotypes do not mean that Democratic women are consistently evaluated in one fashion and Republican women in another. Indeed, in several individual election years, candidate sex was not significantly related to respondent evaluations of congressional candidates. This finding again suggests that the impact of candidate sex, here whether people employ it in their candidate evaluations, is influenced by the conditions of a particular election.

Voting for Women

Voting for a woman is perhaps the ultimate evaluation a voter can make. Even though it may make intuitive sense that certain groups would be more likely to support women candidates with their vote than others, the analysis provides limited support for this notion. In the pooled analysis presented in Chapter 4, women and minorities were more likely to vote for women candidates for the House of Representatives, but neither of these considerations was related to voting for women Senate candidates. Further, the year-by-year analysis indicates that respondent sex and race were only sporadically related to voting for women candidates from 1990 to 2000. Clearly the impact of individual demographic characteristics on choosing a woman candidate is limited, and there is less consistent support for the importance of an "affinity effect" for women voters than earlier research had suggested.

•   •   •

If voter demographics are not key to shaping vote choice for a woman candidate, what is? In this analysis, the major influences, time after time, in determining whether people vote for a woman candidate for Congress was her incumbency status and party correspondence with the voter. Respondents were overwhelmingly likely to choose the woman when she was the incumbent and when she was the candidate of their political party. The impact of these variables dwarfed that of any of the other demographic variables that demonstrated significance. A vast literature on congressional elections tells us that incumbency and political party are the two main influences on vote choice. It is clear from this analysis that these same dynamics influence success for women candidates in the same ways that they do so for men. Given the primacy of political party as a way for people to approach the political world, we should not be surprised that partisan loyalties are not overwhelmed by consideration of a candidate's sex. This conclusion suggests that, whereas voter demographics can potentially exert a limited influence on vote choice for a woman, these effects are small in comparison to the more traditional partisan influences on vote choice.

The same general pattern of other influences being dwarfed by the impact of incumbency and party correspondence is exhibited in the examination in Chapter 5 of the relevance of issues to voting for a woman candidate. A large body of previous research has suggested that people hold clearly stereotyped impressions of the issue capabilities of women and men and that these stereotypes could have a limiting influence on women's chances for success, such as when such issues as defense or the economy are central to voters' concerns. However, more recent work has proposed the idea that people's stereotypes about women's competencies can be a benefit to them if they correspond with what the voters want in that particular election year.

There are two major conclusions from the analysis in Chapter 5. First, there is a very limited role for issues in vote choice involving women candidates. In both the pooled and year-by-year analyses, very few issues were significantly related to voting for women. Instead, as with the analysis of the impact of demographics on vote choice, the most important variables were incumbency and party. So even though issues can have a limited, episodic impact, they do not represent a major component in the voting calculus of most people. From this information we can conclude that issues have a more limited power to hurt, or help, women candidates. It may be the case that voters hold stereotyped ideas about the issues women and men candidates are best suited to handle. But there is less evidence that these stereotyped considerations form a significant part of the vote decision or that they can overwhelm the important influence of party and incumbency.

The other significant finding to note is that issues, although still limited in their impact, were more important in voting in Senate elections than in those for the House. As suggested earlier, this difference makes sense in terms of our more general understanding of House races being low-information elections and Senate races having a greater emphasis on issues. But beyond this project, it could signal to us that the impact of issues may depend, in part, on the level of office being considered. It makes sense that voters would have little issue position information on candidates for lower-level offices, which would make it unlikely that they would shape vote choice. But in more visible statewide elections, such as governor, U.S. Senate, or the presidency, issues will play a more prominent role. Perhaps in these elections we would see a more important role for respondent issue concerns on vote choice and a greater potential for stereotyped ideas about women candidates to have an impact.

Electoral Context

One of the most consistent findings of the analysis conducted for this project is that there are no consistent influences on people's decisions to choose or reject women candidates. There is some limited evidence of an impact for voter characteristics and issue positions, but it is not present in each, or even most, of the six elections under examination. This fact raises questions about the potential importance of the situations and conditions of a particular election to whether people will choose women. I test this general proposition in several ways in Chapter 6. In a broad sense, I treat candidate sex as a piece of information in the electoral environment. People need to be aware of a candidate's sex for it to matter to their vote choice. Of course, awareness of a woman candidate's sex can trigger other potentially relevant considerations, such as gender stereotypes about issues and candidate traits. I suggest then that it is easier for candidate sex to have an impact on voters when there is more gender-related information in the electoral environment.

Clearly, the amount of gendered information in elections is variable across time and, interestingly, does not appear to be a function of the number of women candidates running in a particular election. Instead, circumstances of a particular election year can result in a greater or lesser focus on candidate sex and gender-related information, imparted primarily through the media. As has been stated, the 1992 "Year of the Woman" elections stand as the primary example of an election rich in gendered information.

In looking at House and Senate elections from 1990 to 2000, the analysis indicates that a greater amount of gendered information in the electoral environment is significantly related to voting for women House candidates. The amount of information is particularly important to voters with lower levels of political awareness. This finding suggests that it is easier for people to make the connection between their own interests and women candidates when there is more information available to help them make the connection and that some voters are more dependent on the presence of this information than others. However, we again see the importance of a consideration of the election itself because the amount of gendered information in the environment was not related to voting in Senate races.

The impact of voter characteristics and issue concerns also appears to be conditioned by the amount of gendered information available. Women are more likely to vote for women candidates in more gender-rich elections than in those without a substantial focus on gender issues. The impact of issues is also heightened in these situations. Several issues, such as abortion, defense, and attitudes toward the women's movement, have a stronger impact on voting for a woman candidate when there is more gendered information in the election environment. In most cases, the influence is strongest for voters with lower levels of political awareness. Note that the issues with a greater impact here are those with substantial gender content of their own. It would appear that an electoral environment with a greater emphasis on candidate sex and gendered issues raises the importance of gendered issues in the voting calculus.

Caveats

This book is an attempt to capitalize on currently existing sources of data that allow us, for the first time, to examine the behaviors and attitudes of a large group of voters who have the opportunity to choose between women and men candidates in real-life elections. The findings paint a complex picture of the impact that candidate sex can have on voters, one that is shaped by aspects of the voters, the candidates, and the unique circumstances of an individual election. But we must also recognize that the focus here is exclusively on congressional elections. Unfortunately, available data do not allow for examination of elections for governor, other statewide offices, or state legislative races involving women. Although there is no obvious set of reasons to assume that similar dynamics would not be at work in these races, we must acknowledge that potential differences between congressional and other elections could exist.

More work is needed to examine how voters in actual elections evaluate and choose women for governorships and other state-level races. For elections for governor, exit-poll data from such sources as the Voter News Service could represent a good, if somewhat limited, source of data for such an exploration. State legislative races could also be particularly fruitful because there are more women candidates for these offices than any other. However, conducting similar analysis for state legislative races would require collecting demographic and public opinion data on voters who were faced with women candidates, a task that is no doubt restricted by logistic and financial limitations.

The other issue to acknowledge is the relatively limited time frame covered by this analysis. The past 15 years have seen the greatest increase in the number of women candidates running for Congress. But we will need to examine the findings outlined here into the future to determine if the trends displayed here will continue to shape the public's considerations of women candidates indefinitely.

Conclusion

The analysis presented in this book suggests that, whereas candidate sex does have some impact on voters' attitudes and behaviors in congressional elections, that impact is small compared to more traditional political influences, such as political party and incumbency, and the impact is smaller than some research would indicate. It also suggests that the impact of candidate sex is conditioned by forces in the electoral environment, pointing to a complex interaction of several forces at work in our political world. Clearly, given the opposition women candidates in earlier times faced, the relationship between the public and women who seek elected office has changed tremendously. Gone are the days when the most significant thing about a woman candidate was her sex, which was seen, depending on the time, as a disqualifying characteristic or a charming curiosity. Today, women who run for office are likely to do as well as similarly situated men, whether in gaining party nominations, raising campaign funds, or winning votes from the public.

Yet even as we begin the twenty-first century, candidate sex can still be relevant to elections, and we still refer to them as "women candidates." The public does often view women differently than men, which, depending on the situation, can be a positive or a negative for women. In some circumstances, certain groups of people will be more likely to support women at the polls. One question that must remain unanswered for the present is whether the evolution in the relationship between women candidates and the public is complete or whether changes in the way people perceive women will continue to occur. There are two possible answers to this dilemma. First, the recent evidence of a role for candidate sex may be a reflection of the political relevance of sex (and the related concept of gender) that will not change over time. There is significant evidence to suggest that candidate sex matters because women and men voters exhibit some important differences in their political attitudes and behaviors, whether these differences involve seeking political representation or particular policy outcomes. These differences may stem from a number of sources: socialization, life experience, or differing needs from, and expectations of, government. But, regardless of source, they point to relatively stable differences between women and men that will not necessarily disappear as women become a greater percentage of the candidate pool.

Alternatively, it may be that research finds a role for candidate sex in elections because women are still a relatively new phenomenon on the scene. Although it is true that women have been serving in elected office in the United States for quite some time, until recently they were still something of an oddity. It is only in the last decade or so that women candidates have become numerous enough to gather a critical mass of attention. Because women's integration into political office is a relatively recent, and ongoing, process, our current thinking about the impact of candidate sex on the public, on voters, and on election outcomes may be a function of this time and place in our political history. Put another way, the impact of candidate sex may continue to be a function of their novelty. Perhaps, at some point in the future, women candidates will be seen as candidates who happen to be women as opposed to "women candidates," and their sex will not warrant a second thought.

Notes

1. King, David, and Richard Matland, "Partisanship and the Impact of Candidate Gender in Congressional Elections: Results of an Experiment," paper presented at the Women Transforming Congress conference, Carl Albert Center, University of Oklahoma, 1999.

Appendix A

THE DATA FOR THIS PROJECT COME FROM the National Election Study surveys for 1990 through 2000. Specifically, I use the data from each survey for respondents who lived in a state or congressional district in which a woman ran for the House of Representatives or the Senate in that year. The sample of respondents for each NES survey is a representative cross-section of the American public. The sample universe is all U.S. households (including civilian households on military bases) in the 48 coterminous states and the District of Columbia. The NES employs a multistage area probability design. The first stage randomly selects SMSAs, counties, and county groups. The second stage randomly selects area segments (housing unit clusters defined by census blocks). The third stage randomly samples housing units from the chosen area segments, and the fourth stage randomly selects a respondent from the eligible members in each sample household.[1]

One result of this method is that the NES does not interview people in every state or congressional district (CD) in the country, which means that not every state or CD in which a woman candidate ran is included. Table A.1 presents the data for the number of women candidates whose state or CD was included in each NES survey and the total number of women candidates who ran in that year.

This strategy of surveying means that 46 percent of the women candidates who ran for Congress from 1990 to 2000 ran in districts or CDs that were included in the NES. The data analyzed here, then, represent almost half of the respondents who had the opportunity to choose a woman candidate for Congress during this time period. As stated above, only those respondents who lived in a state or CD with a woman candidate running for Congress are included in the analysis. When the data are pooled, this provides an N of 1,093 respondents for analysis of women candidates for the House of Representatives and 1,296 respondents for women candidates for the Senate.

TABLE A.1:
Number of WC Included in NES Sample and Total Number of WC

	Number of WC included in NES sample	Total Number of WC
1990	28	77
1992	48	117
1994	48	121
1996	70	129
1998*	40	131
2000	95	135
Total	329	710

* The 1998 NES sample was much smaller than any of the others in the time period covered, which results in a smaller number of women candidates being represented in the districts and states sampled.

Notes

1. For more detailed sample information, see http://www.umich.edu/~nes/studyres/datainfo/implement.htm.

Appendix B

THE FOLLOWING ARE THE NES QUESTIONS used to create the variables in this analysis.

Dependent Variables

Vote Choice: A dummy variable that accounts for whether the respondent voted for the woman candidate (1) or not (0).

Perception of House Candidate Ideology: Where would you place the Democratic/Republican House candidate on this scale—1 = extremely liberal, 7 = extremely conservative. (1990: v409/v410; 1994: v843/v844; 1996: v960375/v960377; 1998: v980407/v980409; 2000: v001378a/v001380a. Not asked in 1992.)

Salience Scores: Was there anything in particular that you liked/disliked about the Democratic/Republican candidate for the U.S. House of Representatives? What was that? (5 probes.) Salience scores are created by adding together the total number of things that the respondent said that he or she liked and disliked about each candidate. (1990: v198-v221; 1992: v5401-v5424; 1994: v401-v424; 1996: v961044-v961067; 1998: v980275-v980298; 2000: v001328-v001351.)

Female/Male Issue Mentions: Same question as for salience scores. Here the responses are coded into categories based on substantive issue mentions for traditional female and male issues.

Independent Variables

Respondent Characteristics

Party Identification: Strength of party identification based on a seven-point scale ranging from strong Democrat to strong Republican. (1990: v320; 1992: v3634; 1994: v655; 1996: v960420; 1998: v980339; 2000: v000523.)

Ideology: Self-rated seven-point scale ranging from extremely liberal to extremely conservative. (1990: v406; 1992: v3509; 1994: v839; 1996: v960365; 1998: v980402; 2000: v000447.)

Sex: Respondent sex. (1990: v547; 1992: v4201; 1994: v1434; 1996: v960066; 1998: v980672; 2000: v001029.)

Age: Respondent recoded age. (1990: v552; 1992: v3903; 1994: v1203; 1996: v960605; 1998: v980572; 2000: v000908.)

Race: Respondent race. (1990: v549; 1992: 4202; 1994: v1435; 1996: v960067; 1998: v980673; 2000: v001006a.)

Religiosity: People practice their religion in different ways. Outside of attending religious services, do you pray: 1 = several times a day, 2 = once a day, 3 = a few times a week, 4 = once a week or less, or 5 = never? (1990: v513; 1992: v3822; 1994: v1045; 1996: v960573; 1998: v980494; 2000: v000874.)

Education: Summary of respondent years of education. (1990: v557; 1992: v3908; 1994: v1209; 1996: v960610; 1998: v980577; 2000: v000913.)

Respondent Issue Positions/Attitudes

Defense: Some people believe that we should spend much less money on defense. Others feel that defense spending should be greatly increased. And, of course, some people have opinions somewhere in between. Where would you place yourself on this scale, or haven't you thought much about this? 1 = greatly decrease defense spending, 7 = greatly increase defense spending. (1990: v439; 1992: v3603; 1996: v960463.) Should federal spending on defense be increased, decreased, or kept about the same? (1994: v827; 2000: v000587.)

Social Welfare: Should federal spending on solving the problems of poor people be 1 = increased, 2 = kept about the same, or 3 = decreased? (1992: v3817; 1996: v960565; 2000: v000680. 1990: v382, substituted "food stamps" for "poor people." 1994: v820, substituted "welfare" for "poor people.")

Public Schools: Should federal spending on public schools be 1 = increased, 2 = kept about the same, 3 = decreased. (1990: v383; 1992: v3818; 1994: v823; 1996: v960562; 2000: v000683.)

Abortion: There has been some discussion about abortion during recent years. Which one of the opinions on this page best agrees with your view? The result is a four-point scale where 1 = by law, abortion should never be permitted; 2 = the law should permit abortion only in the case of rape, incest, or when the woman's life is in danger; 3 = the law should permit abortions for reasons other than rape, incest, or danger to the woman's life, but only after the need for the abortion has been clearly established; 4 = by law, a woman should always be able to obtain an abortion as a matter of personal choice. In 1992 only, it was a five-point scale where 5 = R rejects the concept that abortion should be regulated by law; law has nothing to do with it. (1990: v479; 1992: v3732; 1994: v1014; 1996: v960503; 2000: v000694.)

Child Care: Should federal spending on child care be 1 = increased, 2 = kept about the same, 3 = decreased? (1990: v385; 1994: v824; 1996: v960564; 2000: v000685. In 1992 only: v3745—Do you think that 1 = the government should provide child care assistance to low- and middle-income working parents, or 2 = it isn't the government's responsibility?)

Attitudes Toward Feminists/The Women's Movement: Feeling thermometer for "the women's movement" on a scale from 0–100. (1990: v158; 1992: v5324; 1994: v308; 1996: v961039; 2000: v001318.)

Attitudes Toward House Candidates: Feeling thermometer for Democratic and Republican House candidates on a scale from 0–100. (1990: v145/v146; 1992: v5311/v5312; 1994: v238/v239; 1996: v960278/v960279; 1998: v980239/v980240; 2000: v001298/v001299.)

Perception of Party Ideology: Where would you place the Democratic/Republican Party on this scale? 1 = extremely liberal, 7 = extremely conservative. (1990: v413/414; 1992: v3517/v3518; 1994: v847/v848; 1996: v960379/v960380; 1998: v980411/v980412; 2000: v001382/v001383.)

Other Independent Variables

Gender Context: A measure of the amount of sex/gender information about women candidates in the electoral environment. I conducted an analysis of the number of newspaper stories about women candidates that appeared in local and national newspapers from September 1 to the day before the election for each year from 1990 to 2000, with the exception of 1998. The "U.S. News" section of Lexis-Nexis was employed, using the search phrases "women candidates" and "election."

Woman Incumbent: A variable that measures the incumbency status of the woman candidate. Incumbent = 1, open seat = 0, challenger = -1).

Party Correspondence: A variable measuring whether the woman candidate and the respondent were of the same political party.

References

Abramowitz, Alan. 1995. "It's Abortion, Stupid: Policy Voting in the 1992 Presidential Election." *Journal of Politics* 57:176–186.

Abramson, Paul, John Aldrich, and David Rohde. 2002. *Change and Continuity in the 2000 Elections.* Washington, D.C.: CQ Press.

Adams, William. 1975. "Candidate Characteristics, Office of Election, and Voter Responses." *Experimental Study of Politics* 4:76–88.

Aldrich, John, John Sullivan, and Eugene Borgida. 1989. "Foreign Affairs and Issue Voting: Do Presidential Candidates 'Waltz Before a Blind Audience'?" *American Political Science Review* 83:123–141.

Alexander, Deborah, and Kristi Andersen. 1993. "Gender as a Factor in the Attribution of Leadership Traits." *Political Research Quarterly* 46:527–545.

Alvarez, R. Michael, and Jonathan Nagler. 1998. "Economics, Entitlements, and Social Issues: Voter Choice in the 1996 Presidential Election." *American Journal of Political Science* 42:1349–1363.

Andersen, Kristi. 1996. *After Suffrage: Women in Partisan and Electoral Politics Before the New Deal.* Chicago: University of Chicago Press.

Anthony, Susan B., and Ida Harper. 1969. *History of Woman Suffrage.* New York: Arno Press.

Ashmore, Richard, Frances Del Boca, and Arthur Wohlers. 1986. "Gender Stereotypes," in *The Social Psychology of Female-Male Relations: A Critical Analysis of Central Concepts.* Eds. Richard Ashmore and Frances Del Boca. Orlando, Fla.: Academic Press.

Barnello, Michelle. 1999. "Gender and Roll Call Voting in the New York State Assembly." *Women and Politics* 20:77–94.

Becker, Jo, and Dan Balz. 2002. "Tug of War over Women in Maryland's 8th." *The Washington Post*, October 20.

Boles, Janet. 1991. "Advancing the Women's Agenda Within Local Legislatures: The Role of Female Elected Officials," in *Gender and Policymaking: Studies of Women in Office.* Ed. Debra Dodson. New Brunswick, N.J.: Eagleton Institute of Politics, Rutgers University.

Bratton, Kathleen, and Kerry Haynie. 1999. "Agenda-Setting and Legislative Success in State Legislatures: The Effects of Gender and Race." *Journal of Politics* 61:658–679.

Broverman, Inge, Susan Vogel, Donald Broverman, Frank Clarkson, and Paul Rosenkrantz. 1974. "Sex Role Stereotypes: A Current Appraisal." *Journal of Social Issues* 28:59–78.

Brown, Clyde, Neil Heighberger, and Peter Shocket. 1993. "Gender-Based Differences in Perceptions of Male and Female City Council Candidates." *Women and Politics* 13:1–17.

Burrell, Barbara. 1994. *A Woman's Place Is in the House: Campaigning for Congress in the Feminist Era.* Ann Arbor: University of Michigan Press.

Campbell, Angus, Philip Converse, Warren Miller, and Donald Stokes. 1960. *The American Voter.* Ann Arbor: Survey Research Center, University of Michigan.

Carroll, Susan. 1999. "The Disempowerment of the Gender Gap: Soccer Moms and the 1996 Elections." *PS: Political Science and Politics* 32:7–12.

Center for the American Woman and Politics (CAWP). 2000. *Fact Sheet.* "Women in the U.S. Congress." New Brunswick, N.J.: Eagleton Institute of Politics, Rutgers University.

———. 2000. *Fact Sheet.* "Women Candidates for Congress 1974–2000." New Brunswick, N.J.: Eagleton Institute of Politics, Rutgers University.

———. 2000. *Fact Sheet.* "Women Candidates for Congress 1974–2000: Party and Seat Summary for Major Party Nominees." New Brunswick, N.J.: Eagleton Institute of Politics, Rutgers University.

———. 2002. *Fact Sheet.* "Women Candidates in 2002: Congressional and Statewide Office." New Brunswick, N.J.: Eagleton Institute of Politics, Rutgers University.

———. 2002. *Fact Sheet.* "Women in State Legislatures 2002, Women in the U.S. Congress 2002." New Brunswick, N.J.: Eagleton Institute of Politics, Rutgers University.

———. 2002. *Fact Sheet.* "Summary of Women Candidates for Selected Offices 1970–2000." New Brunswick, N.J.: Eagleton Institute of Politics, Rutgers University.

Clarke, Harold, and Marianne Stewart. 1994. "Prospections, Retrospections, and Rationality: The 'Bankers' Model of Presidential Approval Reconsidered." *American Journal of Political Science* 38:1104–1123.

Conover, Pamela, and Stanley Feldman. 1989. "Candidate Perception in an Ambiguous World." *American Journal of Political Science* 33: 912–939.

Converse, Philip. 1962. "Information Flow and the Stability of Partisan Attitudes." *Public Opinion Quarterly* 26:578–599.

Cook, Elizabeth. 1994. "Voter Responses to Women Senate Candidates," in *The Year of the Woman: Myths and Realities.* Eds. Elizabeth Adell Cook, Sue Thomas, and Clyde Wilcox. Boulder: Westview Press.

————. 1998. "Voter Reaction to Women Candidates," in *Women and Elective Office: Past, Present, and Future*. Eds. Sue Thomas and Clyde Wilcox. New York: Oxford University Press.

Costello, Cynthia, and Anne Stone. 2001. *The American Woman 2001–2002*. New York: W. W. Norton.

Dalager, Jon. 1996. "Voters, Issues, and Elections: Are the Candidates' Messages Getting Through?" *Journal of Politics* 58:486–515.

Darcy, R., Susan Welch, and Janet Clark. 1994. *Women, Elections, and Representation*. 2nd ed. Lincoln, Nebr.: University of Nebraska Press.

Delli Carpini, Michael, and Scott Keeter. 1996. *What Americans Know About Politics and Why It Matters*. New Haven: Yale University Press.

Deutsch, Sarah Jane. 2000. "From Ballots to Breadlines: 1920–1940," in *No Small Courage: A History of Women in the United States*. Ed. Nancy Cott. New York: Oxford University Press.

Devitt, James. 2000. *Framing Gender on the Campaign Trail: Women's Executive Leadership and the Press*. Philadelphia: Annenberg Public Policy Center, University of Pennsylvania.

Dinkin, Robert. 1995. *Before Suffrage: Women in Partisan Politics from Colonial Times to 1920*. Westport, Conn.: Greenwood Press.

Dodson, Debra. 1998. "Representing Women's Interests in the U.S. House of Representatives," in *Women and Elective Office: Past, Present, and Future*. Ed. Sue Thomas and Clyde Wilcox. New York: Oxford University Press.

————. 2002. "Acting for Women: Is What Legislators Say, What They Do?" in *The Impact of Women in Public Office*. Ed. Susan Carroll. Bloomington: Indiana University Press.

Dolan, Kathleen. 1997. "Gender Differences in Support for Women Candidates: Is There a Glass Ceiling in American Politics?" *Women and Politics* 17:27–41.

————. 1998. "Voting for Women in the 'Year of the Woman.'" *American Journal of Political Science* 42:272–293.

————. 2001. "Electoral Context, Issues, and Voting for Women in the 1990s." *Women and Politics* 23:21–36.

Downs, Anthony. 1957. *An Economic Theory of Democracy*. New York: Harper.

Deutsch, Sarah Jane. 2000. "From Ballots to Breadlines: 1920–1940," in *No Small Courage: A History of Women in the United States*. Ed. Nancy Cott. New York: Oxford University Press.

Duverger, Maurice. 1955. *The Political Role of Women*. Paris: UNESCO.

Eagly, Alice. 1987. *Sex Differences in Social Behavior: A Social-Role Interpretation*. Hillsdale, N.J.: Erlbaum.

Edwards, Rebecca. 1997. *Angels in the Machinery*. New York: Oxford University Press.

Ekstrand, Laurie, and William Eckert. 1981. "The Impact of Candidate's Sex on Voter Choice." *Western Political Quarterly* 34:78–87.

Feldman, Linda, Francine Kiefer, and James Thurman. 1999. "Dole's Candidacy Has Historic Impact." *Christian Science Monitor*, October 21.

Feldman, Stanley, and Pamela Johnston Conover. 1983. "Candidates, Issues, and Voters: The Role of Inference in Political Perception." *Journal of Politics* 45:810–839.

Fiorina, Morris. 1981. *Retrospective Voting in American National Elections.* New Haven: Yale University Press.

Fiske, Susan, and Steven Neuberg. 1990. "A Continuum of Impression Formation, from Category-Based to Individuating Processes: Influences of Information and Motivation on Attention and Interpretation," in *Advances in Experimental Social Psychology.* Ed. Mark Zanna. San Diego: Academic Press.

Flanigan, William, and Nancy Zingale. 2002. *Political Behavior of the American Electorate.* 10th ed. Washington, D.C.: CQ Press.

Foerstel, Karen. 1998. "For Women Candidates, an Uncertain Season." *CQ Weekly* 56:39.

———. 1999. *Biographical Directory of Congressional Women.* Westport, Conn.: Greenwood Press.

Fox, Richard. 1997. *Gender Dynamics in Congressional Elections.* Thousand Oaks, Calif.: Sage Publications.

Fox, Richard, and Eric R.A.N. Smith. 1998. "The Role of Candidate Sex in Voter Decision-Making." *Political Psychology* 19:405–419.

Frankovic, Kathleen. 1977. "Sex and Voting in the U.S. House of Representatives: 1961–1975." *American Politics Quarterly* 5:315–330.

Freeman, Jo. 2000. *A Room at a Time: How Women Entered Party Politics.* Lanham, Md.: Rowman and Littlefield Press.

Gelman, Andrew, and Gary King. 1993. "Why Are American Election Polls So Variable When Votes Are So Predictable?" *British Journal of Political Science* 23:409–451.

Gertzog, Irwin, and M. Michele Simard. "Women and 'Hopeless' Congressional Candidates: Nominations Frequency, 1916–1978." *American Politics Quarterly* 9:449–466.

Hansen, Susan. 1997. "Talking About Politics: Gender and Contextual Effects on Political Proselytizing." *Journal of Politics* 59:73–103.

Hartmann, Susan. 1982. *The Home Front and Beyond: American Women in the 1940s.* Boston: Twayne Publishers.

Harwood, John, and Gerald Seib. 1997. "Female Democrats Lack Issues That Led to '92 Success." *Wall Street Journal*, Eastern ed., December 9.

Herrnson, Paul. 2000. *Congressional Elections: Campaigning at Home and in Washington.* 3rd ed. Washington, D.C.: CQ Press.

Hershey, Marjorie. 1977. "The Politics of Androgyny: Sex Roles and Attitudes Toward Women in Politics." *American Politics Quarterly* 3:261–287.

Huddy, Leonie, and Nayda Terkildsen. 1993a. "Gender Stereotypes and the Perception of Male and Female Candidates." *American Journal of Political Science* 37:119–147.

———. 1993b. "The Consequences of Gender Stereotypes for Women Candidates at Different Levels and Types of Offices." *Political Research Quarterly* 46:503–525.

Huddy, Leonie, and Teresa Capelos. 2002. "Gender Stereotyping and Candidate Evaluation: Good News and Bad News for Women Politicians," in *The Social Psychology of Politics*. Ed. Victor Ottati et al. New York: Kluwer Academic Press.

Iyengar, Shanto, Nicholas Valentino, Stephen Ansolabehere, and Adam Simon. 1997. "Running as a Woman: Gender Stereotyping in Women's Campaigns," in *Women, Media, and Politics*. New York: Oxford University Press.

Jacobson, Gary. 2001. *The Politics of Congressional Elections*. 5th ed. New York: Longman.

Jamieson, Kathleen Hall. 1995. *The Double Bind: Women and Leadership*. New York, Oxford University Press.

Kahn, Kim. 1992. "Does Being Male Help? An Investigation of the Effects of Candidate Gender and Campaign Coverage on Evaluations of U.S. Senate Candidates." *Journal of Politics* 54:497–517.

———. 1996. *The Political Consequences of Being a Woman: How Stereotypes Influence the Conduct and Consequences of Political Campaigns*. New York: Columbia University Press.

Kaptur, Marcy. 1996. *Women of Congress: A Twentieth-Century Odyssey*. Washington, D.C.: Congressional Quarterly.

Kinder, Donald, Gordon Adams, and Paul Gronke. 1989. "Economics and Politics in the 1984 American Presidential Election." *American Journal of Political Science* 33:491–515.

King, David, and Richard Matland. 1999. "Partisanship and the Impact of Candidate Gender in Congressional Elections: Results of an Experiment." Paper presented at the Women Transforming Congress conference, Carl Albert Center, University of Oklahoma.

Koch, Jeffrey. 1997. "Candidate Gender and Women's Psychological Engagement in Politics." *American Politics Quarterly* 25:118–133.

———. 1999. "Candidate Gender and Assessments of Senate Candidates." *Social Science Quarterly* 80:84–96.

———. 2000. "Do Citizens Apply Gender Stereotypes to Infer Candidates' Ideological Orientations?" *Journal of Politics* 62:414–429.

———. 2002. "Gender Stereotypes and Citizens' Impression of House Candidates Ideological Orientations." *American Journal of Political Science* 46:453–462.

Krasno, Jonathan. 1994. *Challengers, Competition, and Reelection: Comparing House and Senate Elections.* New Haven: Yale University Press.

Krosnik, Jon. 1990. "Americans' Perceptions of Presidential Candidates: A Test of the Projection Hypothesis." *Journal of Social Issues* 46:159–182.

Lazarfeld, Paul, Bernard Berelson, and Hazel Gaudet. 1968. *The People's Choice: How the Voter Makes up His Mind in a Presidential Campaign.* 3rd ed. New York: Columbia University Press.

Leeper, Mark. 1991. "The Impact of Prejudice on Female Candidates: An Experimental Look at Voter Inference." *American Politics Quarterly* 19:248–261.

Lewis, Carolyn. 1999. "Are Women for Women? Feminist and Traditional Values in the Female Electorate." *Women and Politics,* 20:1–28.

Luttbeg, Norman, and Michael Gant. 1995. *American Electoral Behavior: 1952–1992.* Itasca, Ill.: Peacock Publishers.

Macrae, C. Neil, Charles Stangor, and Miles Hewstone. 1996. *Stereotypes and Stereotyping.* London: Guilford Press.

Mansbridge, Jane. 1999. "Should Blacks Represent Blacks and Women Represent Women? A Contingent 'Yes.'" *Journal of Politics* 61:628–657.

Marcus, Gregory, and Philip Converse. 1979. "A Dynamic Simultaneous Equation Model of Electoral Choice." *American Political Science Review* 73:1055–1070.

Matthews, Glenna. 1992. *The Rise of Public Woman.* New York: Oxford University Press.

McDermott, Monika. 1998. "Race and Gender Cues in Low-Information Elections." *Political Research Quarterly* 51:895–918.

————. 1998. "Voting Cues in Low-Information Elections: Candidate Gender as a Social Information Variable in Contemporary United States Elections." *American Journal of Political Science* 41:270–283.

Mezey, Susan Gluck. 1978. "Support for Women's Rights Policy: An Analysis of Local Politicians." *American Politics Quarterly* 6:485–497.

Miller, Warren, and Merrill Shanks. 1996. *The New American Voter.* Cambridge, Mass.: Harvard University Press.

Newport, Frank, David Moore, and Lydia Saad. 1999. "Long Term Gallup Poll Trends: A Portrait of American Public Opinion Through the Century." *Gallup Report,* December 20.

Nie, Norman, Sidney Verba, and John Petrocik. 1976. *The Changing American Voter.* Cambridge, Mass.: Harvard University Press.

Niemi, Richard, and Herbert Weisberg, eds. 2001. *Controversies in Voting Behavior.* 4th edition. Washington, D.C.: CQ Press.

Niven, David. 1998. "Party Elites and Women Candidates: The Shape of Bias." *Women and Politics* 19:57–80.

Page, Benjamin, and Richard Brody. 1972. "Policy Voting and the Electoral Process: The Vietnam War Issue." *American Political Science Review* 66:979–995.

Paolino, Phillip. 1995. "Group-Salient Issues and Group Representation: Support for Women Candidates in the 1992 Senate Elections." *American Journal of Political Science* 39:294–313.

Pitkin, Hanna. 1972. *The Concept of Representation*. Berkeley: University of California Press.

Plutzer, Eric, and John Zipp. 1996. "Identity Politics, Partisanship, and Voting for Women Candidates." *Public Opinion Quarterly* 60:30–57.

Pomper, Gerald. 1975. *Voters' Choice: Varieties of American Electoral Behavior*. New York: Dodd, Mead.

Popkin, Samuel. 1991. *The Reasoning Voter*. Chicago: University of Chicago Press.

———. 1993. "Information Shortcuts and the Reasoning Voter," in *Information, Participation, and Choice: An Economic Theory of Democracy in Perspective*. Ed. Bernard Grofman. Ann Arbor: University of Michigan.

Prewitt, Kenneth. 1970. *The Recruitment of Political Leaders*. Indianapolis: Bobbs-Merrill.

Rahn, Wendy. 1993. "The Role of Partisan Stereotypes in Information Processing About Political Candidates." *American Journal of Political Science* 37:472–496.

Reingold, Beth. 2000. *Representing Women: Sex, Gender and Legislative Behavior in Arizona and California*. Chapel Hill: University of North Carolina Press.

Riggle, Ellen, Penny Miller, Todd G. Shields, and Mitzi Johnson. 1997. "Gender Stereotypes and Decision Context in the Evaluation of Political Candidates." *Women and Politics* 17:69–88.

Rinehart, Sue Tolleson. 1992. *Gender Consciousness and Politics*. New York: Routledge.

Rosenthal, Cindy Simon. 1995. "The Role of Gender in Descriptive Representation." *Political Research Quarterly* 48:599–611.

Rosenwasser, Shirley, and Norma Dean. 1989. "Gender Role and Political Office: Effects of Perceived Masculinity/Femininity of Candidate and Political Office." *Psychology of Women Quarterly* 13:77–85.

Rubin, Alissa. 1994. "1994 Elections Are Looking Like the 'Off-Year' of the Woman." *CQ Weekly*, October 15.

Saint-Germain, Michelle. 1989. "Does Their Difference Make a Difference? The Impact of Women on Public Policy in the Arizona Legislature." *Social Science Quarterly* 70:956–968.

Sanbonmatsu, Kira. 2002. "Gender Stereotypes and Vote Choice." *American Journal of Political Science* 46:20–34.

Sapiro, Virginia. 1981/82. "If U.S. Senator Baker Were a Woman: An Experimental Study of Candidate Images." *Political Psychology* 3:61–83.

Sapiro, Virginia, and Pamela Johnston Conover. 1997. "The Variable Gender Basis of Electoral Politics: Gender and Context in the 1992 US Election." *British Journal of Political Science* 27:523.

Seltzer, Richard, Jody Newman, and Melissa Leighton. 1997. *Sex as a Political Variable: Women as Candidates and Voters in U.S. Elections.* Boulder: Lynne Rienner.

Sigelman, Lee, and Carol Sigelman. 1982. "Sexism, Racism, and Ageism in Voting Behavior: An Experimental Analysis." *Social Psychology Quarterly* 45:263–269.

Sigelman, Lee, and Susan Welch. 1984. "Race, Gender, and Opinion Toward Black and Female Candidates." *Public Opinion Quarterly* 48:467–475.

Silleto, John, and Constance Lieber. 1994. "Martha Maria Hughes Cannon," in *Utah History Encyclopedia.* Ed. Allan Kent Powell. Salt Lake City: University of Utah Press.

Simmons, Wendy. 2001. "A Majority of Americans Say More Women in Political Office Would Be Positive for the Country." *The Gallup Poll Monthly*, January.

Smith, Charles, Peter Radcliffe, and John Kessel. 1999. "The Partisan Choice: Bill Clinton or Bob Dole?" in *Reelection 1996: How America Voted.* Ed. Herbert Weisberg and Janet Box-Steffensmeier. New York: Chatham House.

Smith, Eric R.A.N., and Richard Fox. 2001. "The Electoral Fortunes of Women Candidates for Congress." *Political Research Quarterly* 54:205–221.

Smith, Tom. 1979. "A Study of Trends in the Political Role of Women, 1936–1974," in *Studies of Social Change Since 1948.* Ed. James A. Davis. NONC Report 127B. Chicago: NONC.

Swers, Michele. 2002. *The Difference Women Make: The Policy Impact of Women in Congress.* Chicago: University of Chicago Press.

Thomas, Sue. 1994. *How Women Legislate.* New York: Oxford University Press.

Thomas, Sue, and Susan Welch. 1991. "The Impact of Gender on Activities and Priorities of State Legislators." *Western Political Quarterly* 44:445–456.

Thompson, Seth, and Janie Steckenrider. 1997. "The Relative Irrelevance of Candidate Sex." *Women and Politics* 17:71–92.

Thornton, Arland, Duane Alwin, and Donald Camburn. 1983. "Causes and Consequences of Sex-Role Attitudes and Attitude Change." *American Sociological Review* 42:211–227.

von Baeyer, Carl, Debbie Sherk, and Mark Zanna. 1981. "Impression Management in the Job Interview: When the Female Applicant Meets the Male (Chauvinist) Interviewer." *Personality and Social Psychology Bulletin* 7:45–51.

Welch, Susan. 1985. "Are Women More Liberal Than Men in the U.S. Congress?" *Legislative Studies Quarterly* 10:125–134.

Werner, Emmy. 1968. "Women in the State Legislatures." *Western Political Quarterly* 21:40–50.

Wilcox, Clyde. 1994. "Why Was 1992 the 'Year of the Woman'? Explaining Women's Gains in 1992," in *The Year of the Woman: Myths and Realities.* Eds. Elizabeth Adell Cook, Sue Thomas, and Clyde Wilcox. Boulder: Westview Press.

Williams, John, and Deborah Best. 1990. *Measuring Sex Stereotypes: A Multination Study.* Newbury Park, Calif.: Sage Publications.

Zaller, John. 1987. "The Diffusion of Political Attitudes." *Journal of Personality and Social Psychology* 58:821–837.

————. 1992. *The Nature and Origins of Mass Opinion.* New York: Cambridge University Press.

Zanna, Mark, and Susan Pack. 1975. "On the Self-Fulfilling Nature of Apparent Sex Differences in Behavior." *Journal of Experimental Social Psychology* 11:583–591.

Zipp, John, and Eric Plutzer. 1985. "Gender Differences in Voting for Female Candidates: Evidence from the 1982 Election." *Public Opinion Quarterly* 49:179–197.

Index

Page numbers in bold type indicate tables or figures.